Film Actresses

Volume 9

Bette Davis

Documentary study

Part 1

ISBN-13 : 978-1514219126
ISBN-10 : 1514219123

Notice

This documentary study use historic, archived documents.

Because of this, some pages may look blurry or low quality.

Still are included in this book because they have

high value from critical, documentary, historical,

informative and journalistic point of view .

Dtp
and
graphic design

Iacob Adrian

Author statement

The actors and actresses are the the bricks .

The cast and crew are the plaster .

They stand on the foundation created by
producers and writers and directors .

All these people creates the great palace
of the art of film .

Iacob Adrian - 2013

This little Book conveys the greetings of

....

to

....

_____

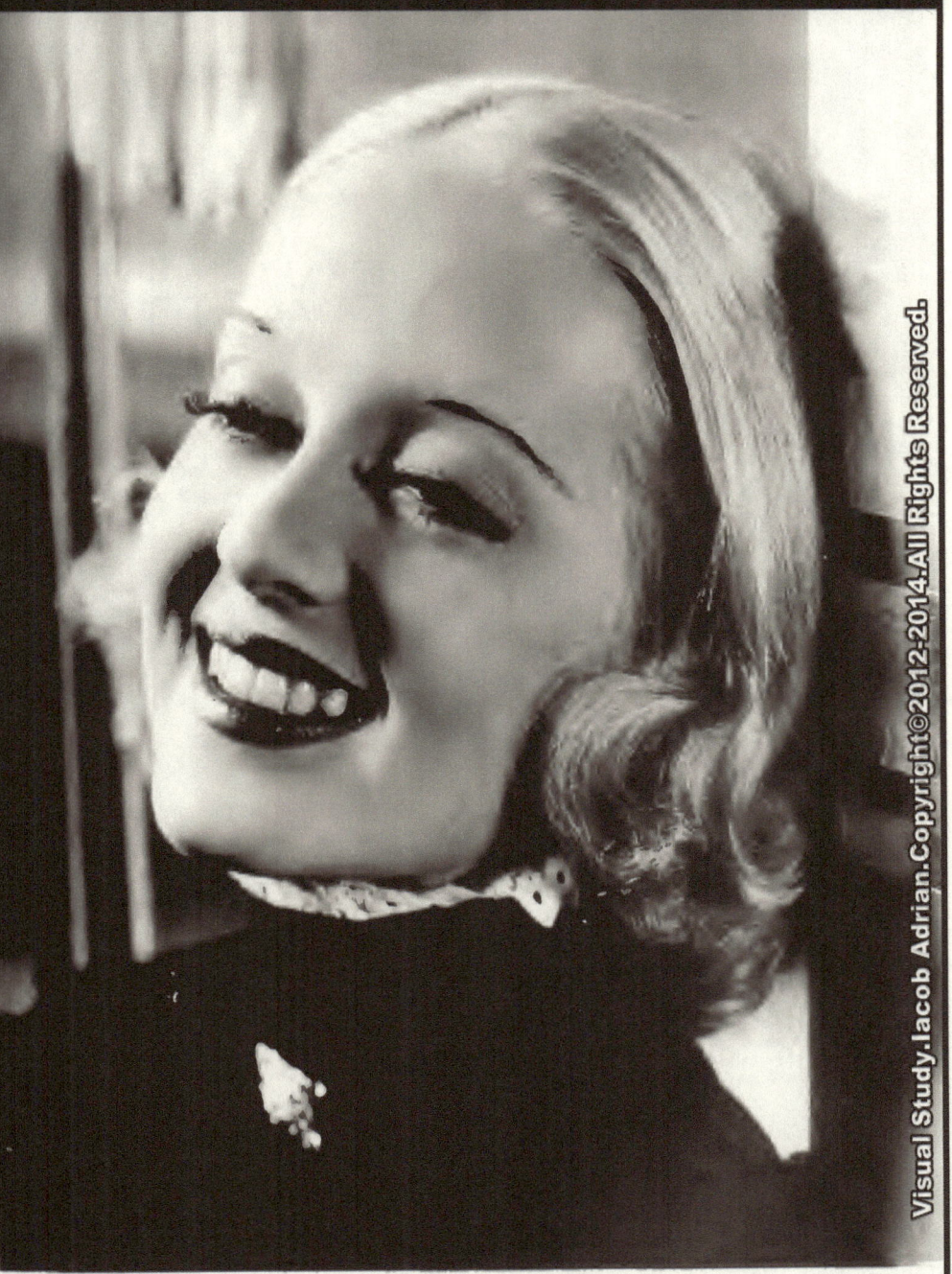

Bert Longworth

BETTE DAVIS—Forgot early desire to be a nurse in high school eagerness for stage career. Studied with John Murray Anderson. Given initial opportunity in George Cukor's stock company. Then to Broadway. Made good in several plays. Hollywood beckoned, and a Universal contract. No luck—option dropped. Bette changed her disposition; turned snappy instead of sweet. A Warner contract and flicker fame! Married to Harmon O. Nelson.

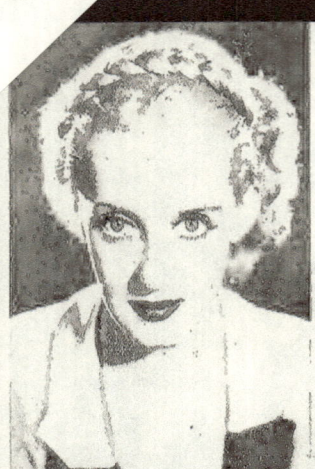

—Scotty Welbourne
Bette Davis declares the detachable braid is the greatest invention since the lipstick

NEW HAIR

DIRECT FROM

by PERC and ERN WESTMORE
Max Factor Studio Makeup Experts

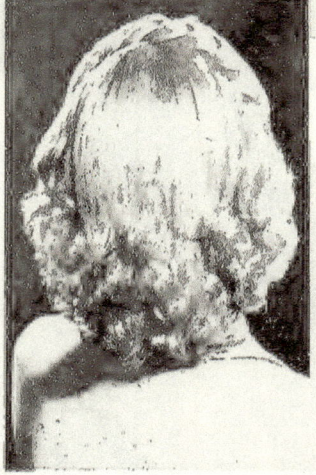

—Scotty Welbourne
Bette's braid is worn across the top of the head and is held in place by invisible elastic

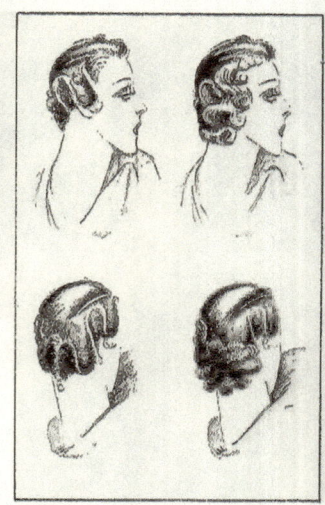

How Norma Shearer's coiffures were designed for Riptide. The curls (shown in the two pictures at the right) are detachable and were applied over loosely waved hair (left)

Summer ... New Gowns ... a brand new hair mode!

What's going to happen to *your* hair this summer? Make it something exciting. Something different. You're going on a vacation. Let your hair go on one too! Change it. Hollywood says: You can glide swiftly from one personality to another with a change of hairdress. The stars are doing it at least three times a day!

Difficult? Not at all. Not when you know the new tricks. Every smart woman knows the idea of wearing hair the same way for every occasion, year in and year out, is deader than yesterday's headline. *Variety.* That's the keynote.

Braids and cluster curls are the two most important features of the latest coiffures.

They add. They give you that irresistible quality called "chic." Bette Davis claims that the braid, detachable and with every hair always in place, is "the greatest invention since the lipstick!"

We made one for her, a shining golden one to match her own hair exactly. "It saves an unbelievable amount of time and bother," she informed us. Yes, and the best part of it is that every girl can get one at any good hairdressing shop. A braid is not expensive. It ought to be from sixteen to eighteen inches long and it'll more than pay for itself in the long run. The point is—you want to be up to the minute with the least trouble. This is the answer.

Bette wears her's across the top of the head and it remains in place with an elastic arrangement which you hide under your hair in back. Then your problem of a formal headdress is solved in a second. Simple—and charming.

Or you can use the braid at an angle—especially if you have a very round face. In that case, part your hair on the left side and start the braid above the right ear and bring it over diagonally to the other side. Where the hair is fullest, attach the braid to it with a clip and wear a similar clip on the opposite shoulder. This not only makes your face seem more slender but gives a girl a definitely vogue-ish air.

Another way is to wear the braid as a neat finish to the back of the hair under your new tilted hat during the day. Or you can coil it on one side of the head and, if you're piquantly young, balance it with curls on the other side.

Kay Francis, like Bette, wears hers straight across. So does Irene Dunne, and Claudette Colbert has been seen with her braid across the back of her head like a coronet.

The main thing to remember is, the newest hair-dos are essentially feminine. Short bobs and conventional set headdresses and bangs are entirely out of date. Hair should be full shoulder length to enable the really smart woman to do it up in several swanky fashions. She starts out in the morning for work or a shopping trip with her hair tailored slightly high about the face and with a gradual dip in back. The ends may be curled tight and close to the face to give that fresh, crisp look.

For afternoon or dinner she combs out the wave more loosely and fluffs the ends—particularly if she's wearing a chiffon dress or anything else as flatteringly feminine. But for evening she abandons the simple coiffure and goes in for elaborate touches if she wants to be in the mode.

STYLES

HOLLYWOOD

● And here is where the additional hair pieces become almost a necessity. Little clusters of puffs and curls have always been considerably intriguing! In the *Riptide* headdress, for example. In doing that for Norma Shearer, we wanted something that stood out as ultra modern. So it was a matter of parting the hair on the side, the usual part is five inches long, giving it a loose diagonal wave and dressing it very high on one side, as well as very full, with tight puffs.

The forehead, of course, is still kept clear. But here's another little device the stars are using. They are cutting their hair an inch back from the hairline in front so they can swirl it without disturbing the back. This gives

New Hair Styles

a delightfully softened appearance to the features.

If a girl has an extreme personality she can do the very unusual and look stunning. Like winding a piece of fabric similar to her evening dress in with her braid. And she can wear what we call the "dual personality" hairdress. That is where the hair is done differently on either side. Comb your long bob straight back on one side as if you were subscribing to the severe boyish headdress of a year or so ago. Then bring it around to the other side and fashion it into a series of flat little curls! All the hair on that side is waved and curled. The front is definitely swirled high on the forehead. A person looking at you first from the right and then from the left side gets two quite distinct impressions of what you're like!

Ingenious, clever, artful—that's the secret of the new coiffure. There's something else to be considered with it. *Make-up.*

Every detail of the face is revealed with these headdresses. Your powder, rouge and lipstick must blend in perfect harmony with your own special coloring or the effect will be completely spoiled. The red of your cheeks should fade away so subtly towards the temples and ears that it defies detection. No trace of powder should be obvious. The hair actually is the frame for the face—and the face should be an interesting picture!

Period pictures are naturally having a tremendous influence on hairdressing. *Catherine the Great* in the persons of Elizabeth Bergner and Marlene Dietrich will bring back the vogue for curls all

over the head. *Du Barry,* interpreted by Dolores Del Rio, revives the pompadour with hanging curls. And Norma Shearer is soon to do *Marie Antoinette.*

Interesting too, to see the results when Katharine Hepburn makes *Joan of Arc.* Will the curls vanish and straight "page" bobs come in again?

OF COURSE EVERY vogue should be adapted to your special needs. No fashionable woman follows it blindly without first duly considering the contour of her face.

If you have a determined chin that looks a bit squarish don't go in for behind-the-car hair arrangements. Let the curls come over your cheeks to soften your profile. A long nose demands that the hair be dressed low to offset it and to give the whole contour of the head a good line. Snubbed noses, however, benefit by high hair-dresses. And if you have a round face be sure to avoid parting your hair in the center.

During the summer, with the dusty country rides and out-door sports and swimming parties, hair should be washed once a week. Use a good mild shampoo and, if your hair is dry, rub olive oil into your scalp a few hours before washing. At the end rinse until the strands separate and feel "loose" in your hands. As often as you can dry your hair by hand. While it's still damp, take an ordinary pencil and wrap paper around it. Then with it wind strands of the hair from the bottom up close to the head, slip out the pencil and keep the hair in place with a hairpin. It will give you a soft lovely wave—without cost!

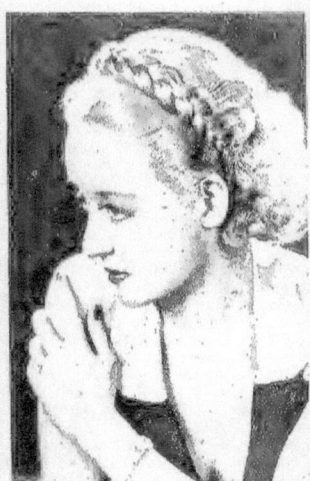

—Scotty Welbourne

A side view of Bette Davis' detachable braid. Braids and cluster curls are the two most important features of the new coiffures

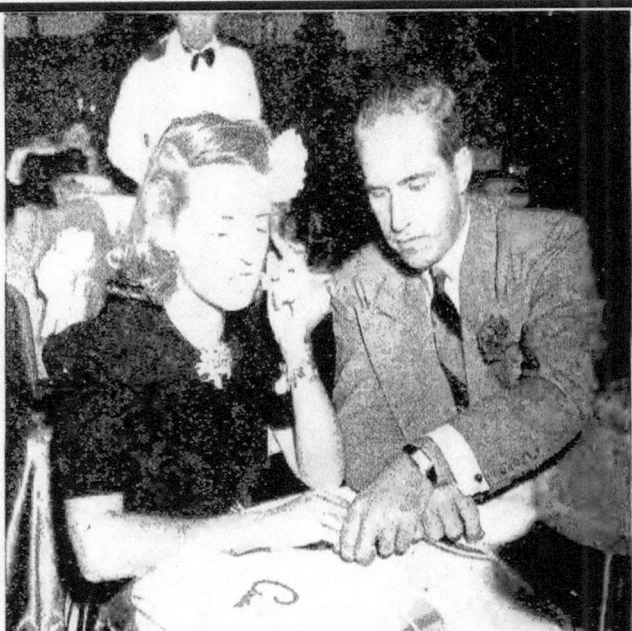

Fawcett photo by Rhodes

Bette Davis has been seen frequently with Bob Taplinger, who is in charge of publicity on the west coast for Warner Brothers' Studios. They vacationed at the same time recently in Honolulu, and here are seen dining in Hollywood at Ciro's

10 Ways to Avoid Divorce —Maybe

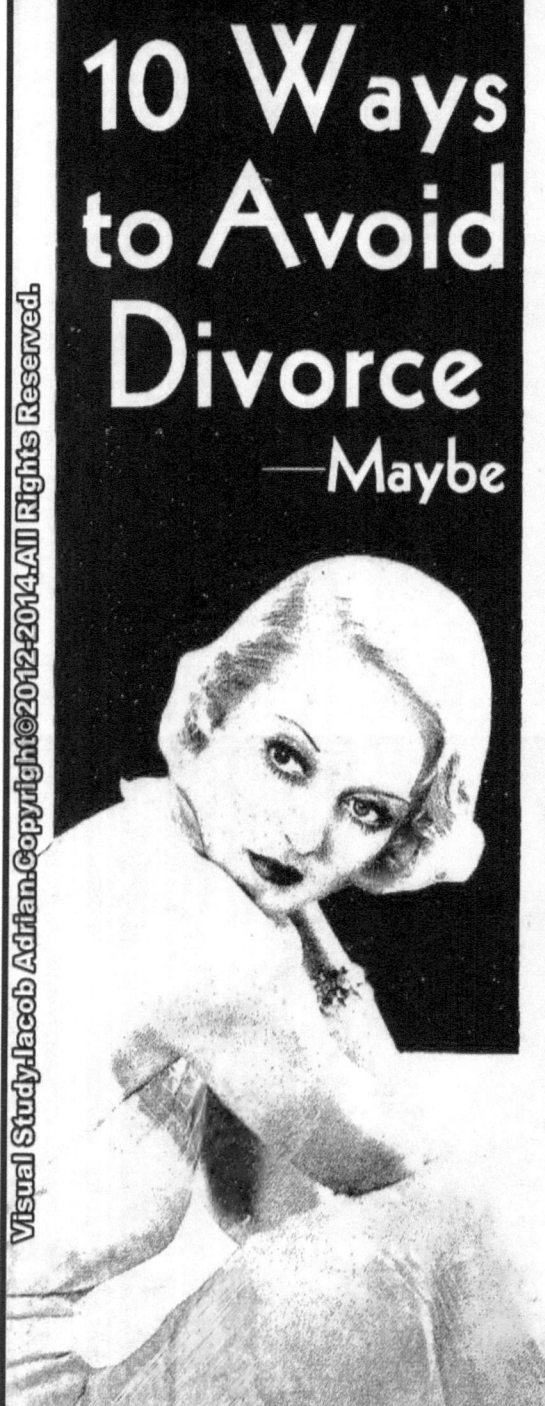

Mrs. Harmon O. Nelson, Jr. has tested them, herself—"and they have worked"

by *Bette Davis*

IN A WAY I am writing this article under protest because I am afraid that you who read it will be thinking, "Who does she imagine she is—the model wife?" I know I'm not! There are days when I do all the things I believe a wife shouldn't, and if my husband reads these thoughts of mine, he will probably groan, "I only wish she would carry them out!" But at least I do know when I'm wrong.

When I was ten years old, you see, my mother and father were divorced. Naturally this has a tremendous effect on a child, and ever since, consciously and unconsciously, I have studied marriage and tried to discover why so many marriages crack up. I formed definite theories on the subject and they have worked out successfully, so far, in my own marriage.

Freedom, I believe, is one of the essentials of a happy marriage. Freedom in big things and freedom in little things. Some wives make a fatal mistake of trying to rule their husbands' lives, and men are dominating creatures who cannot be ruled by anyone! For instance, some women believe that if they allow their husbands freedom to enjoy the companionship of other women, they will lose them. *I believe the exact opposite is true.* A wife can't lose her husband faster than by telling him what to do and whom to go out with. And this works the other way around. If my husband tried to dictate to me, I'd do the very thing he had forbidden—out of spite!

I don't believe there is a married man or woman living who won't meet someone of the opposite sex who is attractive! I know that every now and then I meet a man who intrigues me, and my husband says, "Go ahead and go out with him if you want—it's none of my business!" This is the sensible view. It might make a fatal triangle out of a purely temporary attraction for the husband or wife to stage a scene and command, "Look here, we're married and you've got to stay home!"

I would feel as if I were killing my marriage if I ever did such a thing to Harmon. I married my husband because I love and trust him, and I'm perfectly willing to leave such things to his own discretion. If I kept him from knowing another woman, he might make a big thing out of a little thing, and always have in his heart the feeling, "There's someone I might have been fond of!"

● Fortunately we have more sense about this now than in the days when a momentary attraction was a good reason for divorce. We realize that these fascinations are usually temporary, and don't mean a thing compared to the love a man feels for his wife.

This same idea of freedom applies to all the little things people always tell you are so important in marriage. But you can't realize how important until you're married yourself! My husband and I each have our own work, our amusements, and our friends. We give each other the freedom to retain our separate individualities. He is always after me to learn to play golf with him, but I think it's swell that I don't. It's *right* for him to have his own pleasures in which I have no part. Anyway, women can't really compete with men in sports, and men have to play a different, inferior game when most women are tagging around.

Women shackle their husbands' freedom in other ways—they love making them dress up, even though the average man loathes it. I know of one divorce caused mainly because the wife insisted on her husband dressing for dinner every single night, even when they were alone. Men like to slop around their own homes! My husband feels free to wear whatever he likes, relax, and be comfortable.

Similarly, I would never ask a man to promise me not to do this or that after we're married. You all know girls who boast of "reforming" their husbands. I think that's a fatal mistake. You must make up your mind that the man you marry is going to be just the same kind of man *after* you are married as before. I have seen a girl torture a fellow for two years by asking him not to take the drinks he enjoys. Some day he's going to break out in a wild dash for freedom—and start drinking worse than ever before!

Women, I believe, are usually the worst offenders in marriage. Women are the ones who lead. Women are often more inconsiderate than men. If a woman likes night clubs, the married couple will go to night clubs whether the husband gets a kick out of them or not. But that same woman will fight to keep her husband home from the fishing trips he adores.

If a man likes to go fishing, or if he likes prize fights, I believe he should be encouraged. It makes for separate and distinct individualities, which are so important in marriage. A woman, too, should have some occupation or hobby that is all her own. If possible I believe she should be self-supporting. My husband and I have our own separate incomes and expenses. We are like two independent concerns merged in a sort of partnership. We stay together because we love one another and not because we are tied to each other economically. Even if she doesn't work, a married woman should have some outside interest. It makes for independence as opposed to dependence. I can imagine no more tragic situation than a decent man tied to a woman he no longer loves because she is so utterly dependent on him that he hasn't the heart to ask for divorce. This happens—even in Hollywood!

When Ham and I married, we decided that appreciation would be an important feature of our life together, and I believe this is one good way of avoiding the divorce courts. Too many husbands and wives take little kindnesses for granted, thinking, "Naturally he does nice things for me —he's my husband!" They forget that even a husband enjoys being told!

Consideration is another quality easier to talk about than to put into actual practice. How many men forget that their wives don't give a darn about the details of a business transaction—and come home every night to talk for hours about their various deals? Harmon knows that I know very little about music, and he is considerate enough not to rave on about
Please turn to page eighty-two
MARCH, 1935

10 Ways to Avoid Divorce—Maybe!

the beautiful chord he produced or the applause he got the other night at the Colony.

Sometimes, of course, this can't be helped. It's a natural human impulse to talk about what vitally concerns you. But it can be turned into a pleasant thing simply by bringing the other person actively into the conversation—by *asking their advice*. Incidentally, it is amazingly true that in almost any business worry the advice of an outsider, who knows nothing about the business but who has your best interest at heart, is really valuable.

Ham, for instance, has given me important advice all through my career. At first I didn't want to do *Border Town* because the rôle is another bad-girl type like Mildred in *Of Human Bondage*. Ham convinced me that I should play it because the girl's badness is believable —whereas Mildred's wasn't!—and because if I succeed, it will prove to people that my success in *Bondage* wasn't just a freak of luck.

A really excellent way of avoiding divorce is to go around with happily married couples. If we went around with people who are divorcing, separating, and always swapping husbands and wives, we might very easily reach the foolish point ourselves.

D**IVORCE IS** A**MAZINGLY** tempting to an actress! It means a big splash announcement in the papers, reams of publicity, and being the talk of the town. One could begin thinking that it might be rather *fun*—if you went around with a group in which it was almost contagious!

I am all for divorce, however, if two people really cannot get along. But if there are children, I think it is absolutely wrong. For this reason I don't believe in having children until you've been married three years at least. By that time you should have a good idea as to whether you want to stay married —or not. I have no idea whether I will have children or not. In one way, it's swell to be free to live your own lives when you're young. Responsibility of a family is apt to be a terrific weight on a young husband who is just starting in. On the other hand, if you wait, you may be so much older than your children that it will be even more difficult to bridge the gap of the generations and be a real friend as well as a parent. And this is too valuable a relationship to risk losing.

Keeping romance alive is a favorite topic with writers about happy marriages and how to live them. It has always seemed rather silly to me. I know that when I catch myself making conscious efforts to keep the romance alive in my own marriage, I'll know it must be almost on the rocks.

Perhaps the romance has kept fresh for Ham and me because we both work and one of us is away so much of the time, because we each have our own interests, and because we respect each other's right to his own opinions, friends, and amusements. Which brings me back to where I started, with the belief that the most important thing in marriage is Freedom!

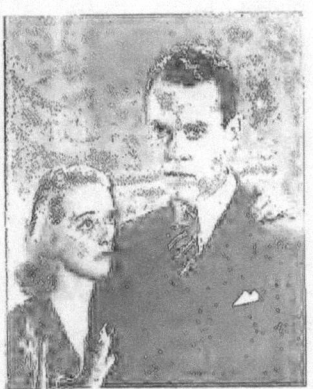

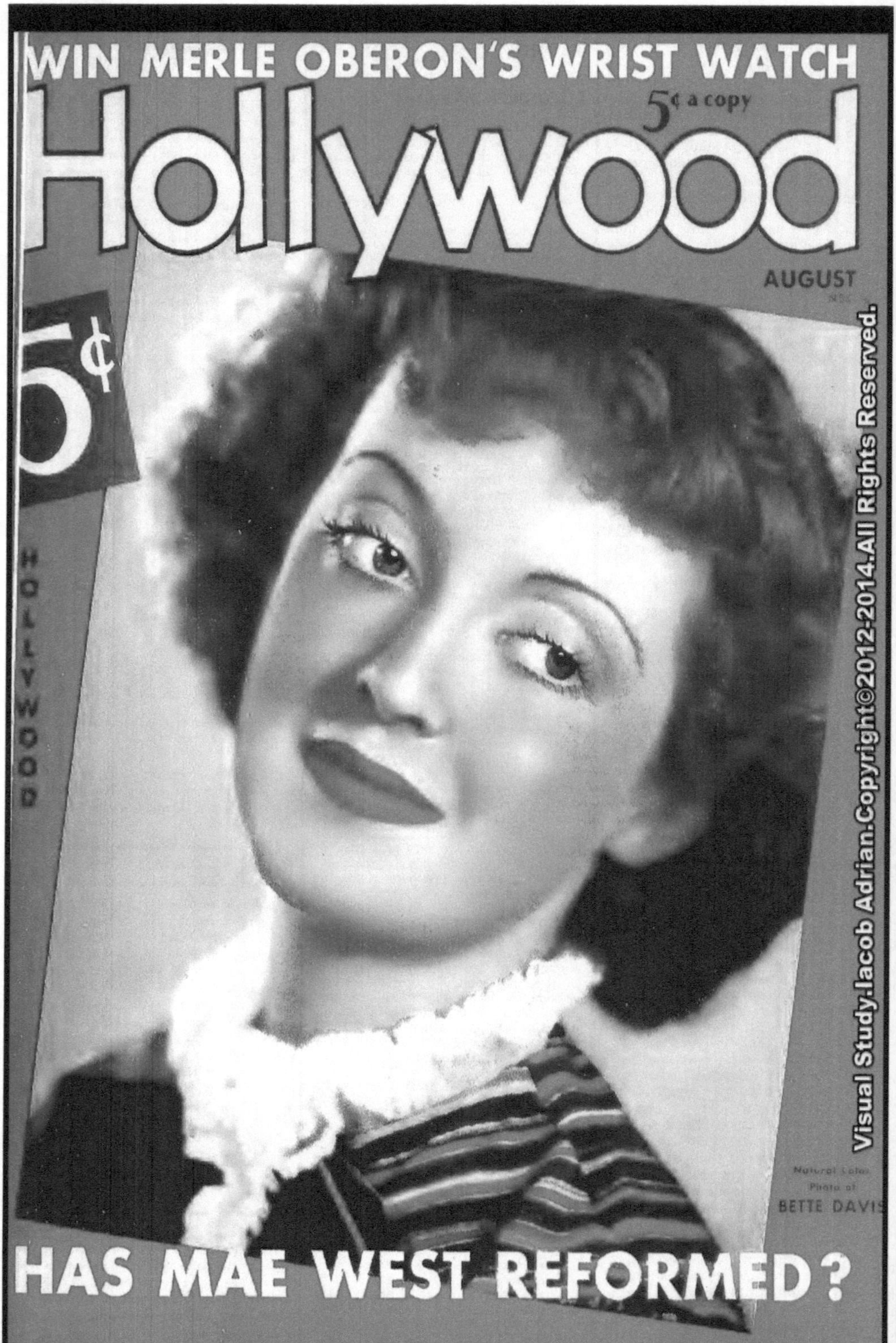

WIN MERLE OBERON'S WRIST WATCH

Hollywood

5¢ a copy

AUGUST

5¢

HOLLYWOOD

Natural Color
Photo of
BETTE DAVIS

HAS MAE WEST REFORMED?

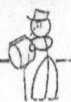

Bette Davis—
Duse of the Dunes

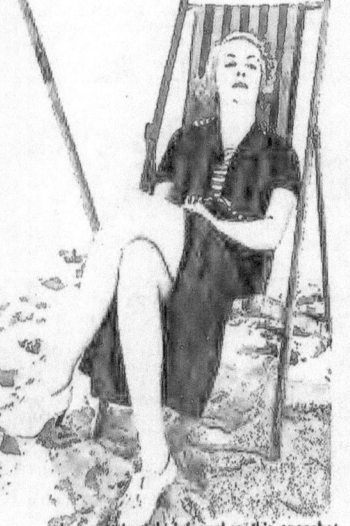

Just as intimately informal as this snapshot is our story about Bette, by a friend

WHENEVER YOU RING the doorbell at Bette Davis' house, you invariably feel a little tinge of nervous excitement; it's rather like that moment before you walk onto a set to play a scene, a mild form of "stage-fright." Upon being ushered into the living-room, where Bette and Harmon O. ("Ham") Nelson are waiting, you always try to "get the jump on them," by asking at once: "Good evening, my chuck, who are we this evening, and where do we live?"

The response to this abrupt greeting is apt to be anything from "How yo'-all, honey-chile" . . . "'Ello, laddie" . . . to "My deah Mr. Watson, chawmed!" That's all the cue that is necessary; then you should know what to expect. Since most of Bette's picture-rôles are "character" and usually dialectic to some degree, she keeps her ear and tongue limber by practicing the speech attitude of her current part.

During the filming of *Cabin in the Cotton*, one almost felt that her Hollywood home had become a house in the "dear old Southland." The most extraordinary period, however, was the *Of Human Bondage* era. To walk into a lovely room, where everything is so tastefully appointed, and to hear a crass cockney-accent being ejaculated was something of a shock as well as very amusing.

This sounds rather "amateurish" and "artistic" when read in print, but Bette has a good reason for this style of vocal and linguistic calisthenics. She has explained it thusly:

"If you have any feeling for dialectics, it isn't very hard to obtain a parrot-like reading of your lines. It just takes practice, but there is always one stumbling-block: you never know when a scene is going to be re-written, and at any time the director may give you some new lines, which you've never seen before.

That sounds logical enough, doesn't it? And it dispels the stigma of "little art theatre" which the reader may have induced.

● A SHORT TIME ago, we went with Bette out to the night-club where Ham's orchestra was playing. We sat at a table

The Kibitzing Caddy » » » » » IRENE DUNNE

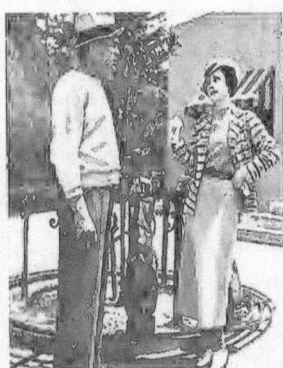

"You look like a strong, silent man. Pick them up, caddy"

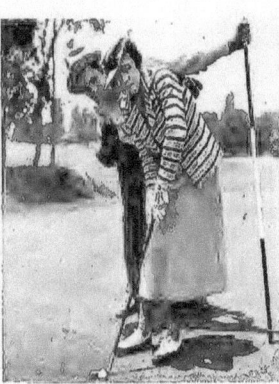

"Haven't I seen you in the movies, lady?"

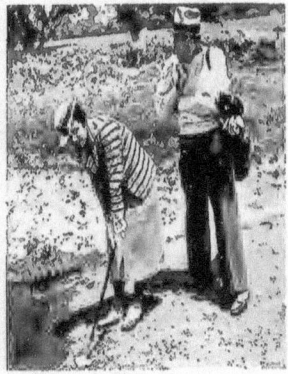

"Say, wat's the name of your latest pictchoor?"

Bette Davis—Duse of the Dunes

near the music, dressed in our best "going-out-to-places" finery. One of Ham's own compositions was being played, and he was about to sing a chorus of the song. We knew better than to indulge in any idle chit-chat at such a moment. We just waited, listened, and watched a lovely young lady, who was enraptured by the performance of her favorite "band-leader!"

One couldn't help thinking, watching this delicately-colored, intense, little sophisticate, of a girl who came into the lobby of the Cape Playhouse, a professional stock company, at Dennis, Cape Cod, seven years ago. The girl upon whom we were musing wore a blue print-dress, and down her back tumbled a cascade of ashen-blond hair, with a tiny blue ribbon tied perkily across the top of her head. We hardly expected to see "Alice," fresh from Wonderland, come walking into the lobby of the rustic theatre by the sea! Rather shyly she spoke: "Could you tell me where we can find a place to live? My mother, sister, cat, and all of our worldly possessions are piled in that Chevvie out there, and we'd like to get settled!" And so we all started out to comb the dunes to find a home for the Davises.

Two hours later they were "dug-in." After all the unloading and arranging had been accomplished, the four of us (the cat had left on a tour of inspection) flopped down to rest, and get acquainted. Without too much modesty Miss Betty (this was before we knew how to spell it) informed us that she was an actress.

To receive your first stock training in a company which boasted casts containing such names as Peggy Wood, Alice Brady, Basil Rathbone, and Henry Hull among many, is very good fortune indeed. And so, until her break arrived, Bette agreed to usher in the theatre at night, and walk on in the mob-scenes, if needed. Humble crumbs they may be, but what sweet bread to the beginner! Nor was she the only young one who fluttered about the playhouse like a moth; the Cape seemed full of them that summer.

● MR. RAYMOND MOORE, the manager, made the suggestion that the earnest young Thespians do a play, and take it on tour about the Cape, under the sponsorship of the Cape Playhouse. It would not only be good training, but it would also advertise the Playhouse. The piece selected for this venture was *The Charm School.* Bette played the leading feminine part. A shy young Englishman who suffered effusive embarrassment during the love scenes, played opposite her.

At four o'clock in the afternoon the unit would strap scenery and props on the top of an antiquated Buick (an investment of thirty dollars), and stuff the cast in any place where it would fit. Looking like a disreputable band of gypsies, it boiled off to a neighboring hamlet, to inflict its golden talents upon the local tax-payers.

The company p l a y e d town-halls, church auxiliary rooms, or school gymnasiums, wherever there was room enough to allow anyone who was patient enough to sit there and watch! The scarcity of stages made it necessary to arrange picnic-sup-

per tables on saw-horses, and to play upon them. Such innovated platforms had a variety of draw-backs; they rattled with every step; they squeaked and shifted at the most inopportune moments; and the company was always very nervous during the big scene in the Second Act when the entire unit of fourteen (14—count 'em—14) was on the stage. At any moment they expected to go crashing through to the floor of the building; luckily they never did.

The only mishap of that tour occurred one night when Bette and a girl named Helen Spaulding sat on the sofa at the same time. The legs broke, and the sofa toppled over backwards. Need one relate the effect this had upon the audience? Several young boys in the first row clambered up on the stage, helped the ladies to their feet, straightened the sofa, and returned politely to their seats in the front row . . . and the performance went on!

● THAT EPOCH-MAKING tour of *The Charm School* terminated in early August, because there were no more villages left on Cape Cod, to invade. Shortly after this Bette got her first real break—the rôle of Dinah, in *Mr. Pim Passes By,* starring Laura Hope Crews. The part called for Dinah to sing an old English song, called "I Passed by Your Window." While Bette rehearsed, Mrs. Davis scoured the Cape for a copy of that song. Mrs. Davis, by some strange coincidence, fell into conversation with an elderly gentleman in Hyannis; he turned out to be the organist in a church in that town, and he had a copy of the coveted song at his home! Every evening Bette rehearsal the song, accompanied by the nice gentleman, in a quaint little old New England church.

The opening-night of *Mr. Pim Passes By* is still a live topic at the Davis camp. At three o'clock in the afternoon Bette was convinced that she had lost her voice, had forgotten all her lines, and was going to be seized with some insidious plague. Bette wasn't able to eat a thing at supper, but Mrs. Davis, whose good sense and judgment has always prevailed, compelled her to peck jitterishly at bowls of corn-flakes, with blueberries and cream! From that auspicious moment this delectable dish has become a traditional opening-night repast for Bette. Whether or not one is superstitious, corn-flakes with blueberries and cream are too good to ignore!

Somehow Bette managed to scramble into "Junior," the Buick and get to the Playhouse. All the way she kept quaking and mumbling: "I can't do it! I know I'll be awful! I won't be able to think of a line! I'll bet my voice cracks!" No amount of comforting would appease her state.

By the time the curtain had rung down, everyone knew that Bette had clicked. It was the start of a great career that inevitably was to lead her from such comparatively minor professional stage work to stardom in the movies.

Bette has soared to the heights, but even now, when the sun sinks down over the blue Pacific near Hollywood, she often thinks of Cape Cod and the Playhouse—days now far distant in yesteryear, but still very close to her heart.

—W. W. WATSON.

No Wonder Franchot Tone
calls BETTE DAVIS

"DANGEROUS"

LOOK WHAT SHE SAYS, IN HER LATEST PICTURE. ABOUT LIFE, LOVE, MEN!

In their first film together

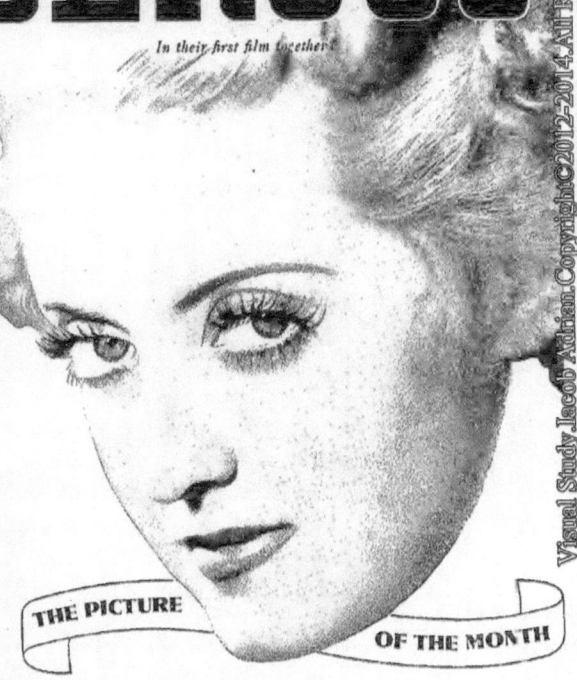

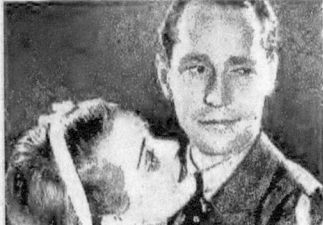

"I'm not lady enough to lie! Loving me is like shaking hands with the devil—the worst kind of luck. But you'll find I'm the woman you'll always come back to!"

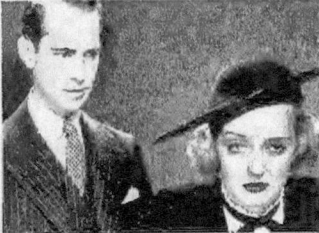

"I've never had any pity for men like you. You with your fat little soul and smug face! Why I've lived more in a day than you'll ever dare live."

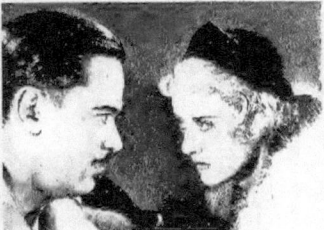

"It's going to be your life or mine! If you're killed, I'll be free . . . If I'm killed, it won't matter any longer . . . and if we both die—good riddance."

THE PICTURE OF THE MONTH

YESSIR, "Dangerous" is the label Franchot tags on the screen's famous blonde temptress. And that's the title Warner Bros. have selected for their first picture together!

If you thought Bette gave men a piece of her mind in "Of Human Bondage", "Bordertown", and "Front Page Woman", wait 'til you hear her cut loose as "the woman men always come back to", in "*Dangerous*".

The way she talks about them—particularly about Mr. Tone —is going to be the talk of movie-fan gatherings. Maybe you'll say she's right when you see what men did to her life. But you'll *certainly* agree that this story of a woman whose love was a jinx to men, is the surprise package of the New Year.

Besides Bette and Franchot, Margaret Lindsay, Alison Skipworth, John Eldredge, and Dick Foran are smartly spotted in a big cast directed by Alfred E. Green. There's no use telling you you *must* see "Dangerous" Because you may not be able to get through the crowds to the box-office when the news of this daring drama gets around town!

My Daughter Bette, by Mrs. Davis

ONE DAY, not so very long ago, I happened to overhear a gentleman talking of Bette.

"She's most unusual," he said, "she uses her head. I'll wager there never was a part written that she wouldn't tackle. She's absolutely fearless when it comes to drama."

no part in the social lives of grown people until they were old enough to take an intelligent part. At times it seemed a bit severe to exclude our two little girls, Bette and Barbara, from the dinner table simply because they weren't old enough to make perfect dinner companions. Now that I look back, I realize that he was

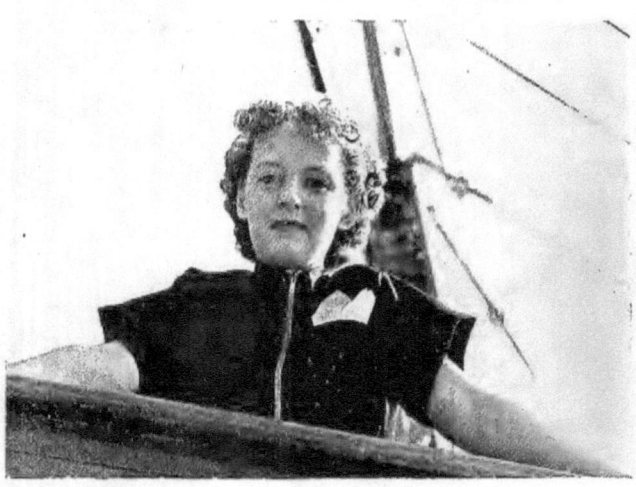

She's the Academy prize winner to you, but only a grown up little girl to Mrs. Davis

My mind flew back over the years, pausing over the events of her life, and in summing up those events, I realized that Bette had always used her head, and that she had always been undaunted and fearless in her effort to forge ahead. Perhaps that quality in her character is a heritage, handed down to her by her forebears who crossed the Atlantic in the *Mayflower* and who took as their symbol of strength, the *Plymouth Rock* upon which they stood as they pledged their faith to God and the new country.

Although some people today place little faith in family and background, I have always believed that Bette was endowed with the spirit of those Pilgrim fathers. Just as they fought off the obstacles of a new country, Bette has fought off all the obstacles connected with her career—and just as they conquered, she conquered. Often afraid and discouraged, she never revealed it to anyone but myself. When the Academy awarded her its highest honor, it was the crowning climax of a long struggle. Thrilled? Of course she was!

● THE FIRST SEVEN years of her life were spent in the typical New England home, devoid of maudlin sentiment, but never lacking in thoughtful kindness. Bette's father believed that children should not rule the home and should take

right from both standpoints—theirs and ours.

We did not turn the house over to the children and adjust our lives to suit their moods. We treated them as people rather than babies and they responded to the treatment. They never heard, and therefore, never uttered a word of baby-talk.

My mother was a great influence in their lives. She always placed common sense ahead of custom and was far ahead of her day. She had polished hardwood floors in her house when every one else had carpets from wall to wall. As a little girl, I wore bloomers to match my dresses when all other little girls were wearing starched white panties trimmed with handmade lace. From my mother, Bette learned to love flowers and to arrange them beautifully. She also learned about birds and all other little outdoor creatures.

When Bette was seven and Barbara six, our home broke up. I felt that a home that was not complete was not a home at all and the question of what would be best for the girls confronted me.

Since they had never been robust children, I sought a country school, becoming very much interested in one in the Birkshire Hills, a *Crestalban* out-door school conducted by Abbot Thayer's sister, Miss Whiting.

My Daughter, Bette

was just about to send out a searching squad when she walked proudly but wearily into the house.

"Well," she said, "I'll either be in high school tomorrow or I won't be."

She had gone to the principal and asked to take the high school entrance examinations. He told her that four of them had already been taken and that she could not take them all at one sitting and that he could not permit her to leave the room while taking them because she might talk to the other children.

● SHE BARGAINED WITH HIM to permit her to take them provided she did not leave her desk until they were all completed. She sat from eight in the morning until after five at night—but she passed and the next day entered high school.

Bette had always been interested in the drama but did not study it seriously until she went to *Cushing Academy* at Ashburnham, Mass. There she studied every phase of it and received actual practice by playing in school plays. It was there that she met Harmon O. Nelson, Junior, who was to become her future husband.

She was sixteen then and they were very much in love. It is characteristic of Bette that she should stay in love with the same man all through the years until she finally married—seven years later. I remember when she came to Hollywood, so many people said, "Well, that'll be the last of Ham." But they didn't know Bette. No matter how many men came into her life, in her heart, it was always Ham.

After Bette finished at *Cushing*, she was determined to have a stage career and I was more than anxious to help her achieve her goal. Barbara had decided upon a University education so that left me to aid Bette in her venture.

We had some hair-raising experiences during the time Bette was struggling to get a foothold. I worked, just as I had ever since our home was broken up, not because I *had* to, but because I loved the work and extra money is always needed when you are trying to bring up children.

We did endure plenty of hardships but the wolf was never 'howling at the door.' We never went without food and we never slept in the park. However, had we been forced to do that, I am sure we would have laughed and considered it a glorious adventure, just as we considered all the other obstacles we had to overcome.

● I THINK THE HARDEST part of those early days rested with Bette. There seems to be so much hopeless, endless waiting connected with getting a part on the stage. I did not have to go through that because I had my daily work but I am sure that Bette often felt impatient, although she never once showed signs of discouragement.

When Bette was sixteen she saw Peg Entrusite play *Hedvig* with Blanche Yurka in *The Wild Duck* and she prayed to do the part. Years later, her chance came, and with it—came the *measles*. For a time it looked as if the opportunity she had so long hoped for was to pass her by.

I said to her, "Now let's figure how soon you *will* be able to play it and maybe they will wait."

It wasn't easy to estimate how soon one might get over an illness but we set the limit at three weeks and they agreed to wait that long. That meant that Bette

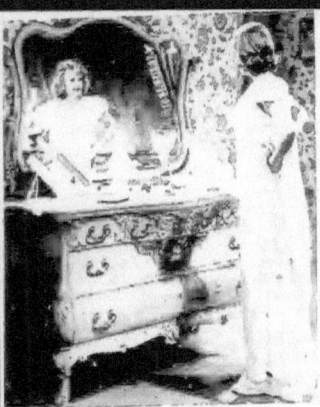

The latest in nightgowns? Well, not exactly! Margaret Sullavan remodels this ancient number during a moment of need in Wanger's *The Moon's Our Home*

Little Success Stories
OF THE STARS.

No. 3   BETTE DAVIS

In which she reveals how she finally "found herself"

by J. EUGENE CHRISMAN

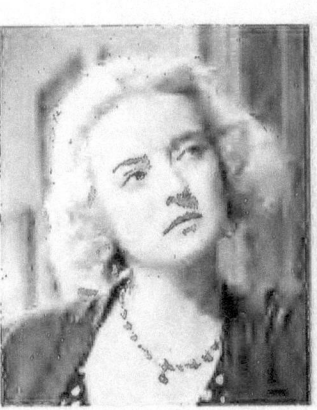

Bette Davis in *Of Human Bondage*

would have to learn her lines by that time also. That girl actually learned that entire difficult part from my reading the lines to her while she was in bed. You see, she could not read because in measles the eyes are weakened and must be protected from any strain.

She was very weak the night she went on and I did hold my breath until the final curtain, feeding her milk and wine between scenes to give her strength. And after it was all over, what do you suppose she said? She said, "Well, Ruth *we* did it!"

Do I have to say more to tell you what kind of a *daughter* she is?

When Bette decided to make Hollywood her home, she began looking around for a house. The new, modern homes in Beverly Hills, Bel-Air, Brentwood, Toluca Lake did not appeal to her. She drove up one street and down the other searching for something that looked like "home."

At last she decided upon a very old house on Franklin Avenue. It looked pretty dingy to me but a month later it was a bit of old New England with all its simple charm. The living room is not large but it is cozy with its fire place and handy book shelves, and it is brightened by many a tiny bowl filled with flowers.

Here Mr. and Mrs. Harmon O. Nelson, Junior, spend their happy evenings doing the things they like best—reading or listening to music.

Up until the time Bette married, we had been together constantly—not so much as mother and daughter, but as good, understanding friends. It was difficult for me to adjust my life without Bette but being a good friend, instead of a sensitive mother, I was happy she was married to the boy she had loved so long.

The friendship we have enjoyed so many years still exists. I have no unreasonable ideas about "duty to mother" and do not feel injured if Bette does not call up every day at a certain hour. I know she'll call when she has time and that when she does it will be because she wants to and not because she feels that it is her "duty," and that knowledge probably makes me the happiest mother in the world. The fact that she is a screen star, winner of the Academy Award for 1935, makes no difference whatever.

"WHEN I CAME out to Hollywood, I didn't expect to last more than two months. I came from Broadway, but I was a shy, timid little thing, so nervous and frightened, of Hollywood when I made *Bad Sister* and *Seed* that I just knew they wouldn't want me."

It was Bette Davis speaking, the little girl who had just electrified Hollywood by her amazing portrayal of Mildred, the little cockney slattern in *Of Human Bondage*. Critics who saw the preview pronounce it one of the really great performances of the screen and it is freely predicted that Warner Brothers, to whom she is under contract, intend to make her a full-fledged star.

Those who met Bette when she first came to Hollywood detected something of the electric sparkle which her timidity and bewilderment could only partly conceal. This came definitely to light when she was cast as the storekeeper's daughter in *Cabin In The Cotton* with Richard Barthelmess. Then followed a succession of rôles for Warner's which, while excellent, failed to bring Bette the distinction she coveted.

"An executive at Universal almost broke my spirit," smiles Bette, "when he told me that I had no more sex appeal than Slim Summerville. I cried for days. I think my trip with the Warner Brothers' *Forty-Second Street* special did more to give me the self-confidence I needed than anything else. I began to realize then, for the first time, that the public was interested in the picture, the final product, and not what went into the making of it. When I returned I decided to quit worrying about the trivial annoyances whether or not the director and producer liked my work. I realized that if I pleased the public they would have to have me."

They will tell you that Bette faced screen oblivion at the time she was selected for the rôle in *Of Human Bondage*. When she walked out on Warners a few months ago in protest over what she termed "dumb dame" rôles and over being assigned a twelve line part as a secretary, the girl for the Leslie Howard picture had not been selected.

"I did many rôles I did not like," she admits, "and *Of Human Bondage* was made before *Housewife*, but it was not released and nobody knew that I would be a hit. It had been agreed that if I took a rôle in *Housewife*, which I thought was unsuited for me, I would be given something good for my next. There it was already filmed in the picture with Leslie Howard and nobody even suspected it, much less myself!"

Several girls turned down the rôle in *Of Human Bondage* and even Leslie Howard himself did not approve of Bette for the rôle but now, gentleman that he is, he frankly admits his mistake.

Another thing which Bette feels has helped give her self-confidence is her marriage to Harmon Nelson:

"It was all just a matter of learning not to subdue or conceal the person who was really me," she confided. "I am really very much like I am on the screen, but I was afraid that people would laugh and call me silly. My marriage has done wonders for me. It became a release for me. At home with Harmon, I began to let go, to let myself be myself, and he encouraged me. I really don't think of being a part of the picture business. I never drag my job into my home."

WATCH FOR ANOTHER LITTLE SUCCESS STORY
NEXT MONTH

Glamorous Bette—

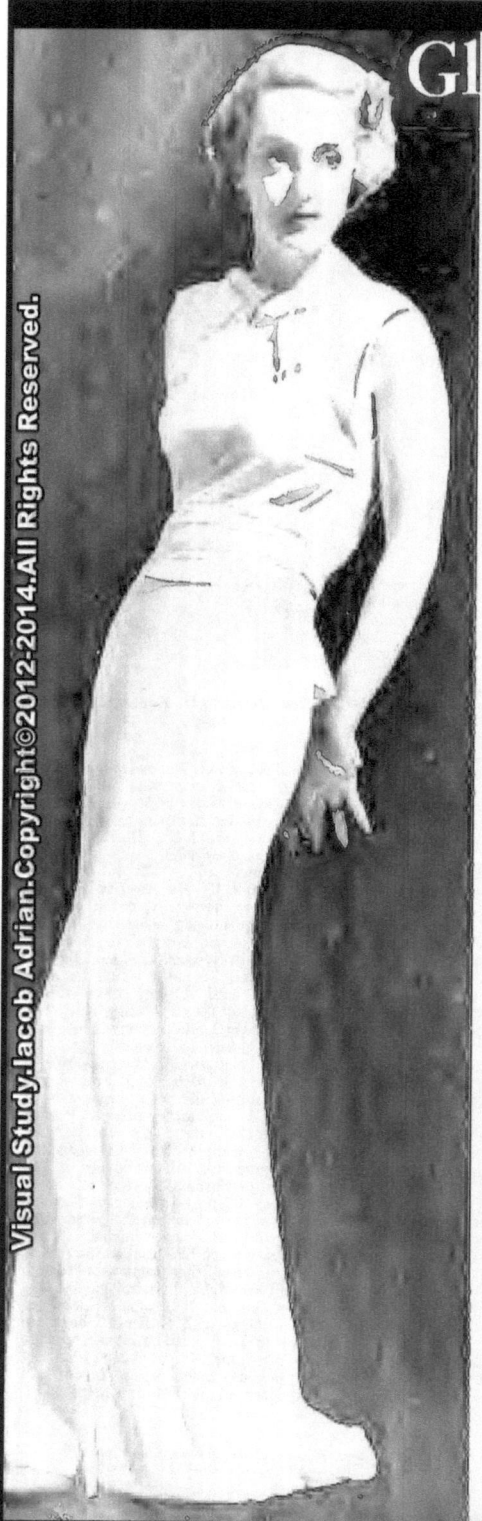

THE GATEMAN's hand trembled as he lifted the receiver of his telephone to call the front office. Dilated with shock, his eyes followed the big car that carried a little bandage-swathed figure down the lot.

"Bette Davis has been horribly hurt!" he croaked into the mouthpiece.

Those words were the raw material for several fine nervous collapses in various parts of the Warner Brothers lot. Miss Davis was right in the middle of shooting *Marked Woman*. A short delay would mean the loss of thousands of dollars to the studio. A serious accident to the star might mean that a fortune in film would have to be scrapped.

The big car drew up before the door of Hal Wallis, Associate Executive in charge of Production. Watchers breathed sighs of relief when they saw that Miss Davis could walk, but they shuddered when they saw her face—or what portions of it showed under the heavy weight of bandages. Both of her eyes seemed swollen, and about to turn black. A brown abrasion promised days of disfigurement for one cheek. A bloody wound was indicated under the white gauze on the other. And her nose! Surely it must be broken to rate such a mountain of cotton and adhesive tape!

Hal Wallis is not a heartless man, but he took one look at the pitiful figure before him, and burst into a roar of laughter! Could he be having hysterics, wondered the shaken by-standers. Strong men sometimes react in surprising fashions to disaster.

Wallis laughed and laughed, but his amusement was completely light-hearted.

"Okay!" he roared. "You get your way . . . all except that broken nose . . . you can't have that. But if you can stand the rest of it, we can!"

A little stiff grimace of echoing amusement was all that the star could manage in the confining gauze.

"Why don't you like the broken nose?" she demanded. "I think it's a wonderful broken nose."

"It's just too much of a good thing," said Wallis, relapsing into another series of chuckles. "Try it without, and you'll see."

"And he was right," Bette Davis said over the luncheon table a few days later. "I look quite convincingly beaten up without a nose bandage. I look AWFUL! I look perfectly FRIGHTFUL! You must see the make-up tests. They are WONDERFUL! You never saw anybody looking worse than I do!"

Her description of her appalling make-up was tinged with genuine delight.

"You see," she explained, "if you really care about acting, you don't care a thing about looking pretty all of the time—it just isn't important. And this is such a marvelous opportunity for realism. In *Marked Woman* I play a dance hall hostess. In the first part of the picture, she has plenty of chances to look attractive. Then she defies the gangsters who control the night club business, and she gets brutally beaten up. She has enough on the gang, so that they are afraid of her, and when they go after her, they stop at nothing. One of her lines is, "They jumped on me . . . they kicked me in the face . . .!"

Miss Davis let that sentence have its full effect while she buttered a roll.

"I never have been kicked in the face, myself," she said, "but my imagination tells me that I would get a good deal more than concussion. Perc Westmore is a grand make-up artist, and he thought he was doing me a favor by putting on a becoming bandage. It was a very becoming turban-like affair, rather nunlike, plenty of mascara and eye make-up. So I argued and argued, and they kept saying, 'But, look, Miss Davis, remember that you are the star of this picture, and people don't want to see you all banged up!'"

She shrugged her shoulders, and a twinkle came into her eyes.

"So you know what I did? I had a morning off, just before the big hospital scene. Lloyd Bacon, the director, believes in realism just as much as I do, so he knew what I had in mind, but not another soul knew.

"I went down town to Dr. Noyes. 'Look,' I said to him. 'Will you fix me up so that they would admit me in a hurry to any emergency ward?'"

Dr. Noyes fell in with the plan enthusiastically, for Miss Davis' pleasure in an unusual make-up is contagious.

First he built a lop-sided hunk of bandage out over one ear. It was anchored by a band that cut slant-wise across her forehead, pulling one eye slightly out of shape.

"This is where you got kicked," he said, and painted an angry looking bruise on one cheek bone.

"Wouldn't my teeth cut my lip?" asked the star.

"Certainly would!" agreed Dr. Noyes, and pulled one side of her mouth down in an angry red line.

"The very first thing that would get broken in a really competent

Marked Woman

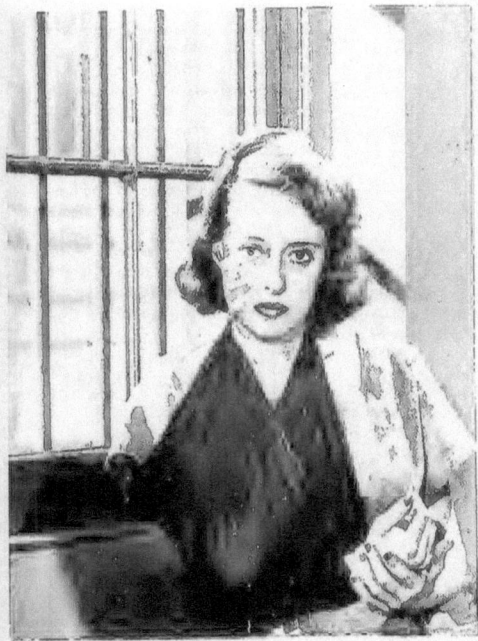

Still photos of Bette as she appeared in the film right after a beating were frowned upon by her studio, so here she is after she has partially recovered, still wearing a facial dressing and carrying her bruised arm in a sling

beating-up would be her nose, wouldn't it?" asked Miss Davis. "Can't I have a broken nose?"

"Why not?" said Dr. Noyes, and got out the splints. "And wouldn't you have to have a bad cut on your hand . . . as if you had reached up to save your face when you saw the knife?" So he put on a mitt of bandage, and threw in a sling for good measure.

"And the scar he put on my cheek was wonderful!" this most remarkable of stars beamed at the memory. "Do you know what he used? Undertaker's wax! You know how there is a sort of ridge on a scar when they first take out the stitches? And how it is all inflamed and drawn? Well, he started by building up that ridge, smoothing it into my cheek. Then he painted it. I don't believe a better scar ever has been seen than that one!"

The conspirators took all morning. When neither one of them could think of another injury to add, Miss Davis sighed with pleasure. The session with Dr. Noyes had been purely experimental on her part, but when she saw the result, she reached a quick decision.

"I'm not going to take this off!" she announced. I'm going to the studio right now, and show them."

In her sense of achievement, she did not stop to realize what a shock her appearance would be.

"I wouldn't have done it deliberately," she said. "But it worked out all right and, though that broken nose bandage was very effective, it really was too much.

"Dr. Noyes had fixed me up to look convincing, but after Perc Westmore had finished fixing me up so that all of those injuries would photograph, you never saw such a face! It's grand!"

"What will you fans think when they see it?"

She leaned forward earnestly. "They'll like it. I know they'll like it. Because it has a look of reality about it. Everybody will know that it is a make-up, of course. But it has the effect of being real, and it gives the part just that much more effectiveness. Awful things happen in this world. *Marked Woman* is a story of what could happen to one girl who was just a little bit too smart for her own good. My conviction is that the people who like my pictures also like realism. And it seems much more important to me to play a real character than just a nicely made-up face.

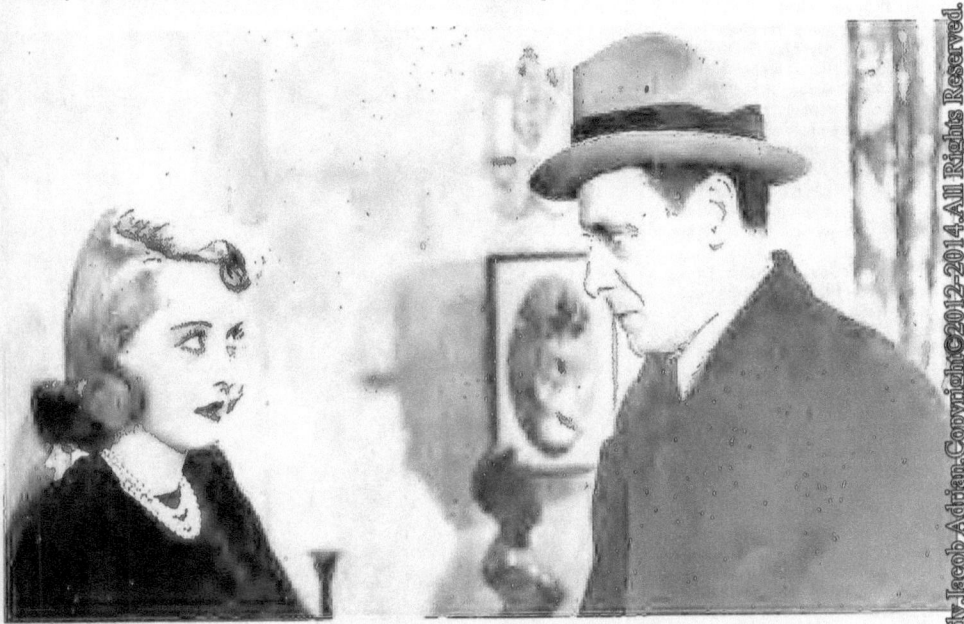

Eduardo Ciannelli, who plays the vice lord in *Marked Woman*, is the underworld fiend who administers the terrific beating to Bette Davis. It is this rough treatment that she felt demanded realism even at the sacrifice of glamour

THE SCREEN'S BEST

BETTE

*Contrary to gossip, Bette Davis is not the great
star determined to have her own way regardless
of others—she's as "regular" as a trouper*

By ARTHUR JANISCH

WOULD you believe that Bette
Davis spends her spare time
pinching tender plants to see
them shrink and wither, scowling
fiendishly at gentle old ladies, and
making babies cry?

Of course not, yet—some people
seem to think that the reason Bette
makes such a success of roles like that
in *Of Human Bondage* is because that
is the way she is in real life!

Bette Davis, more so, perhaps, than
any other star in Hollywood is un-
changed by the roles she portrays on
the screen.

She would not, could not, be the
great actress she is if she were like her
screen characters in real life.

Authority for that statement is none
other than Paul Muni.

"One must look at the character he
is to portray," says Muni, "with the de-
tached, analytical viewpoint of the
intelligent observer. A real thief on
stage or screen would not look like a
real thief. He would not be an actor;
he does not understand why he is a
thief. The actor analyzes the character of the thief; he is great as an actor
because he can project the personality of the thief over that of his own
personality.

"It is ridiculous to assume that an
actor in real life is like the character
he portrays. Being an actor, he discards his character when he discards
his make-up. Were he not to do this
he would not be an actor and there is
no place on stage or screen for those
who are not actors."

Bette Davis is a fiery individual, determined in her likes and dislikes, yet
kind and considerate.

A NEW man assigned to work on
one of Bette's pictures often is
ready to admit that he is prepared to
dislike her. Bette is not unpopular in
Hollywood, but Hollywood is a city of
gossip and legends. Her contract dis-
agreement with Warner Bros. studio—
which cost her at least $50,000—now
happily settled to the satisfaction of all
concerned—and other things occasionally are distorted to the detriment
of Bette.

But the new man meets Bette, con-
vinces her he is a "regular" and comes
back extolling her praises.

To return to her acting ability—she
looks at all pictures with a keen,
analytical mind. If things are not to
her liking she gets what she wants by
her determination which knows no obstacles. She is not the great star
determined to have her own way regardless of the rights of her demands;
invariably she is right, as all who have
worked with her will testify.

In *That Certain Woman*, she portrayed a secretary in the smart offices
of a dignified corporation. It was
decided that Bette was to wear her hair
in a page boy's bob, smooth and sleek
with the

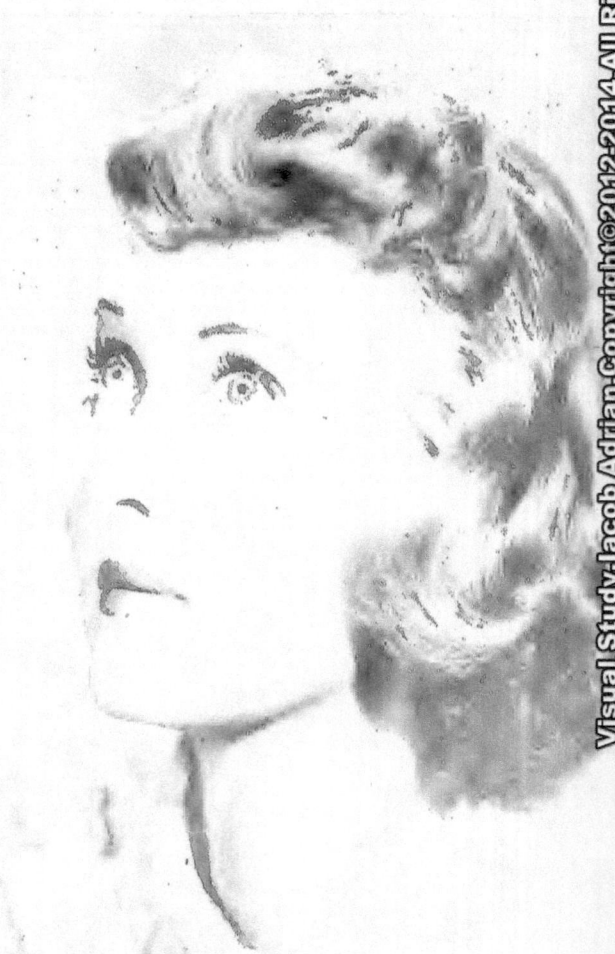

The Screen's Best Bette

ends turned under—until Bette heard about it.

"Nothing doing," she said. "If I came to work with my hair fixed like that in those dignified offices I'd be fired so quick my head would swim."

Director Edmund Goulding saw the wisdom of Bette's reasoning and she wore a hairdress in keeping with the scene.

A STUDIO worker dropped into the wardrobe department at the moment the head was giving some instructions to an assistant.

"She wants those mules and sandals dyed to match her robe," said the wardrobe head. "In those scenes she is going to wear the mules when she gets up and the sandals later on when she is lounging. She says no one would put on sandals when she got out of bed and that it would not be proper to wear mules while she is lounging—"

"Don't tell me," said the studio worker, striking an exaggerated pose. "You're talking about Bette Davis."

"Right," said the wardrobe head.

It would have been equally obvious to anyone else who knew Bette Davis intimately—for only Bette Davis pays such close attention to what, to others, might seem inconsequential details in the delineation of a character.

THE casual visitor to *That Certain Woman* set might have seen Bette painstakingly manicuring and applying enamel to her finger nails. And that casual visitor might have been subjected to a casual inspection by Bette's great eyes.

Bette is not giving herself a manicure to deprive someone of a job, for a make-up man, a hairdresser, and her personal maid is on the set at all times. She is giving herself a manicure because she enjoys it.

Bette Davis is, in real life, as much unlike her screen roles as—sunlight is like a cloudy day.

Sally Sage, who has been her standin for nearly four years, knows her better than anybody with the exception, perhaps, of Harmon Nelson, her husband. Harmon recently gave up a profitable

career as an orchestra leader, incidentally, to be with Bette in Hollywood and is now enjoying great success in the agency business.

Harmon and Bette long since have learned to laugh at Hollywood and its cruelties. Not since the time they exchanged an expensive car for a flivver and were accused of doing it as a publicity stunt have they taken Hollywood seriously.

Sally Sage sees Bette at her best and at her worst. She knows what it is to have Bette standin for her—Bette's standin—when the standin is physically unable to work.

She also knows what it is to be scolded by Bette for being negligent in her duties as standin—such as being absent from the set when Bette needs all her energy for a forthcoming scene but has to standin for herself. She also knows what it means to be encouraged by Bette to better herself, for Bette is giving her elocution and drama lessons and endeavoring to fit her for a career as an actress. But Sally Sage is so satisfied to be just Bette Davis' standin that she cares little about becoming an actress.

Sally Sage belongs to the I'm In Love With Bette Davis Club.

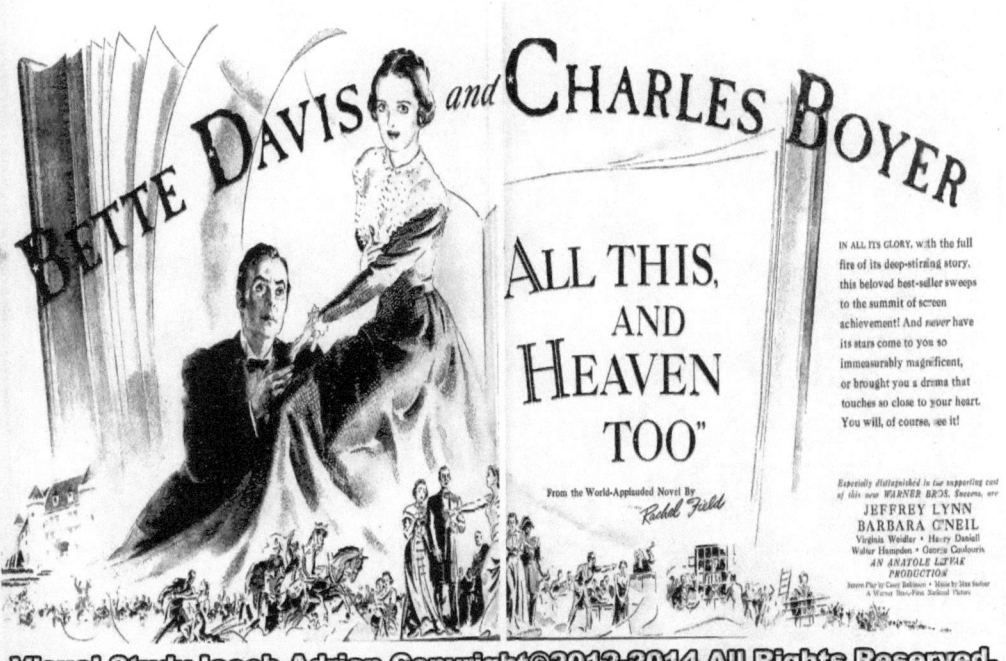

"SPANKINGS SOOTHE THE SOUL"
—SAYS BETTE DAVIS

who believes that one of the best civilizing influences in America today is the good old invitation to see the good old woodshed

By RUTH RANKIN

■ In her latest picture, *That Certain Woman*, Bette Davis plays the mother of a four-year-old boy; her first mother role on the screen.

A discussion of the picture, one recent afternoon, and of her experience at playing mother, led naturally to a hypothetical child of her own. If or when there is ever a little Bette Davis Nelson, or Harmon O. Nelson, Jr., or both, Bette is prepared to take the situation in hand with that intelligent directness for which she is celebrated. . . .

■ We will now take a quick hurdle over that old theory about the women who have no children being the ones who can tell you best how to bring 'em up. But don't be *too* quick, because any theory is liable to explode. The observations of mothers are apt to be limited to their own child or children, while theoretical

mothers have a much wider range. They are not nearly so prejudiced. They have had ample opportunity to witness, with unbiased eye, the mistakes and successes of their friends; which friends are, of course, ambushed in droves hardly able to contain themselves until the time when Madame Now-If-I-Had-A-Child will be practicing her theories. It is always a matter of great astonishment to them, you tell me why, when she turns out to be a good mother.

It will no doubt be a matter of great astonishment to *you* to discover most of Bette's theories to be the sane-and-sensible old-fashioned variety. Which is perfectly logical. Any girl who had the advantage of a good New England upbringing would hardly be expected to advance ultra-modern ideologies.

This speaks well for Bette's own childhood—to any psychologist, even to ama-

teurs like most of us. If she had been sternly sat upon, repressed, inhibited, more than likely she would be one of the most enthusiastic advocates of the new school of child culture which says, in effect, no impulse should be thwarted, no child should be made to do anything he doesn't want to do—and above all, no *spankings*.

■ "No spankings, my eye!" Bette exclaims with her characteristic speak-up manner. "There seems to be an alternation-of-generations principle applied to child-rearing. One generation wallops them, so the next is a bunch of softies, and so on. Well, no generation can afford to neglect the civilizing influence of a good spanking. Children are natural little savages who will get away with all they can. If they are not taught discipline and

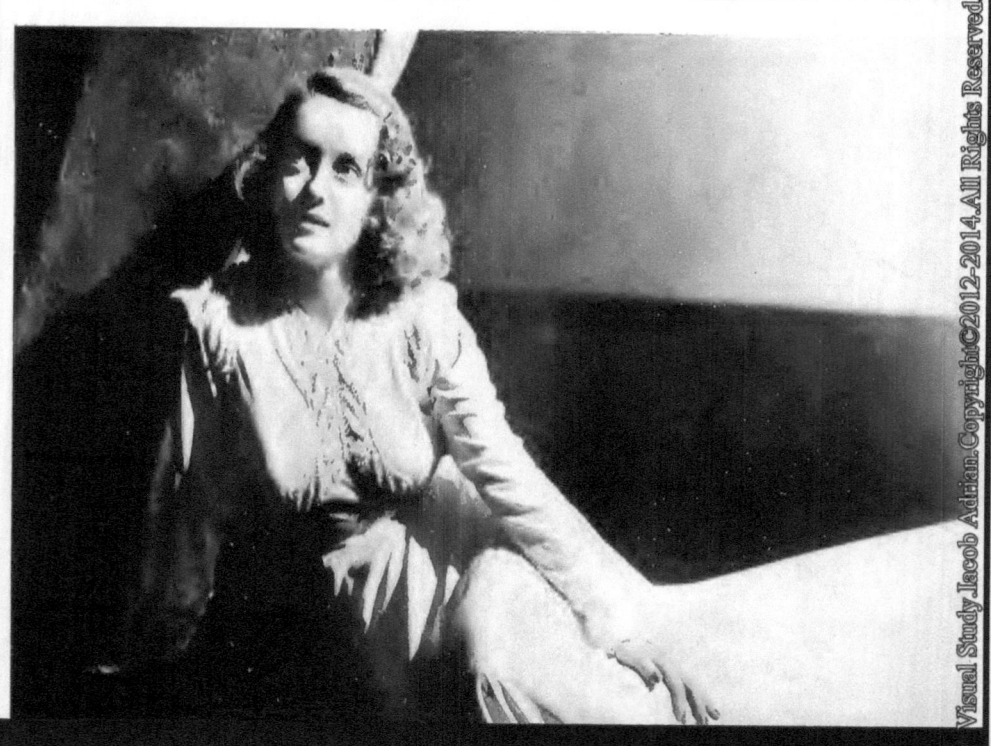

"Spankings Soothe the Soul"

control at home then the world will teach them later, and it will be a much tougher lesson.

"Personally, I should have been spanked a lot more than I was. It would have helped control a perfectly vile temper," said Bette, looking angelic. "I would lie on the floor and kick and scream with all my strength. If my father had been around after I was ten years old (the time when he and my mother were separated) he would have done something about it. Ham's father had a few sessions in the woodshed with *him*; the result is that he can be in a boiling rage and you'd never know it. I have yet to see him lose his temper.

"It is a very hard thing for one parent alone, especially a mother, to bring up children, and all the more credit to my mother for doing as well by Bobbie (Bette's sister) and me as she did.

"We learned independence at an early age. Mother was working and could not be with us very much of the time, so she had to leave certain things to our judgment and common sense—after giving us a good groundwork in both.

"I think children respond to routine and responsibility. They do not enjoy a lack of discipline. If you have never

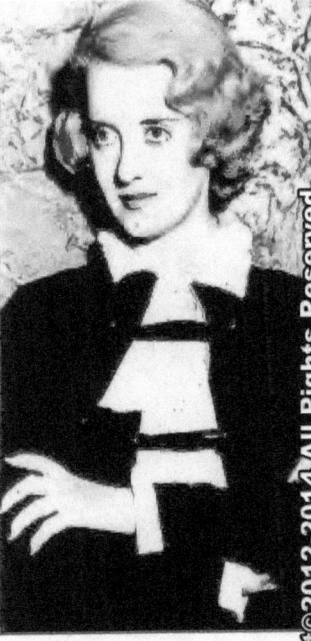

been taught to do what you do not want to do, when you get out in the world and have to for the first time, how do you cope with it? Must be pretty grim for some of the present-day ultra progressives.

"Bobbie and I traveled alone on the train to see our father from the time we were ten. At nineteen, I went to dramatic school alone in New York. Mother said, 'If you can't take care of yourself now, all my training has been for nothing.' I got along very well, and all her training had not been for nothing. But had I been wrenched from the side of an all-shielding protecting silver-cord sort of mother, I would have been in a fine fog. Or from a mother who had never required me to do anything I didn't want to do, or had not thwarted a few of my impulses of which I had plenty of all kinds.

"I have one real theory about children: treat them like grown-ups. A child is a person without benefit of experience; but a person who has learned all the fundamentals necessary to shape his character by the time he is ten years old.

"Children are much more intelligent than the average person realizes. Adults are too prone to be influenced by size. I

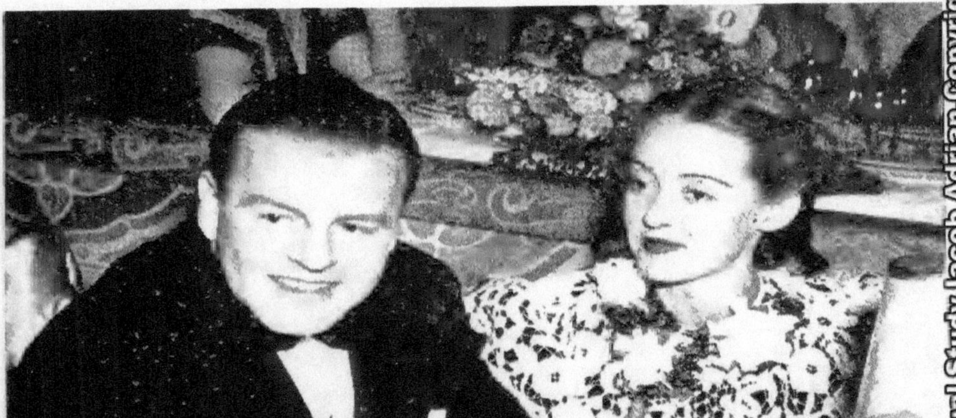

Bette Davis took an old friend from Boston, Arthur Farnsworth, to the Screen Actors' Ball. Notice her hair-do, rolled back like a school-child's from a center part

have met children four feet tall who were more interesting conversationalists than some men six feet tall.

"Two mistakes I have most frequently observed among parents: the sin of bribery, and the holy horror of telling children they are attractive.

"There is no earthly reason why a child should have to be bribed to eat his dinner or take a bath. On the other hand, they should be rewarded for extra duties such as doing the dishes or raking the lawn, if this has been agreed upon in the beginning. An early realization of the value of money seems to me very important.

"Also, I see no reason why a child shouldn't be brought up with an accurate evaluation of his or her own appearance so it will be taken for granted, and not make them self-conscious, vain, or shy, when they meet the world. There was some kind of a phobia in the elder generation against paying compliments to a child. My grandmother typified it perfectly when she always said: 'Now my dear, if you act as well as you look, you'll be all right.' Leaving me with the feeling that there was some doubt about both, but nothing much I could do about it.

■ "Mother was given to harmless flattery, never carried too far. Just enough to give us confidence. And that seems to me one of the most important qualities with which to arm your child. The world will try to take it out of him soon enough, so you can afford to bestow an extra large endowment at home. There has been an awful lot of loose talk going around about the 'self-confidence of youth.' It is simply a defense, in most cases, to cover an alarming lack of it.

"Plenty of praise for children is my platform. Not meaningless or undeserved, but a lot of things could be modestly praised that often go unnoticed.

"The same thing could go for schoolteachers too.

"And speaking of school: I have read a lot of discussion pro and con about teaching sex knowledge in school. Of course the place for children to learn what is called the facts of life, is right at home, from their mothers and fathers. But if actually there are parents who neglect or evade this vitally important subject, then it seems to me better that children learn from a qualified person than get distorted ideas from other children. When they discover their facts this way, mother is pretty apt to be regarded as a coward afraid of the truth, or as a smug reactionary left over from the bustle era. In the end, she forfeits a lot of the respect of her children.

■ "And that," exclaimed Mrs. Nelson, triumphantly — reaching for the afghan she is knitting somebody's baby, "is quite enough to involve me in a controversy with all the mothers in the land!"

"Ah, yes, but just a minute! They grow up and go to high school. What then?"

"That's another department," Bette countered neatly. "They are no longer children, at least not to hear them tell it. Anyway, I'll say this much. The public school system of tests is all wrong. That

has been one of my favorite peeves for years. A thorough teacher shouldn't need tests to know who is good and who isn't. Lots of youngsters go all to pieces and can't do a thing in an exam, when they know the subject perfectly.

There was a short pause. "Oh, to be a child again," I murmured, idly.

"Oh, go jump in the lake!" shrieked Bette who had maintained a painfully ladylike demeanor throughout this discussion. "Who said anything about being a child again? I probably had a childhood far more happy than the average, but I wouldn't go through that again for anything on earth!" Even the planes and prisms in her jewelled clip shot out indignant sparks.

"Only a congenital idiot yearns for his childhood, or an incurable adolescent, or one who has made a complete mess of adult life. So, of course, they are filled with maundering escapist wishes backward to a childhood which probably had no discipline or responsibilities. Nobody with a grain of sense wants to go back to that chaotic time when the world was a whirling frenzy of facts and ourselves trying desperately to reach out and grab a place for ourselves. When all was confusion and bewilderment and impatience, and things were much too slow and to-morrow never came. When we didn't know a doggone thing and made it harder by thinking we knew it all. . . .

"No, thank you. Every interval in life has its own compensations and nothing is so deadly as to go back, even though it is good to have pleasant memories of each interval. But to live in the past is to admit you have no future.

"I would see to it that any child of mine had a childhood as happy as I could possibly give, without neglecting the very important fact that childhood is a preparation for a busy and useful life, and not entirely for having fun."

With which the lady who talks the best mother we have ever heard in a long time folded up her baby-blanket, drank her tea, and departed. A few minutes later, I pried our six-year-old loose from what was left of a chocolate cake—and took Bette's advice on page 33.

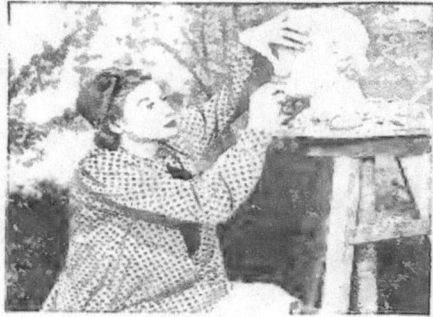

In between shots of *Having a Wonderful Time*, in which she is playing at Radio, Lucille Ball has a good time working on her career as a sculptress

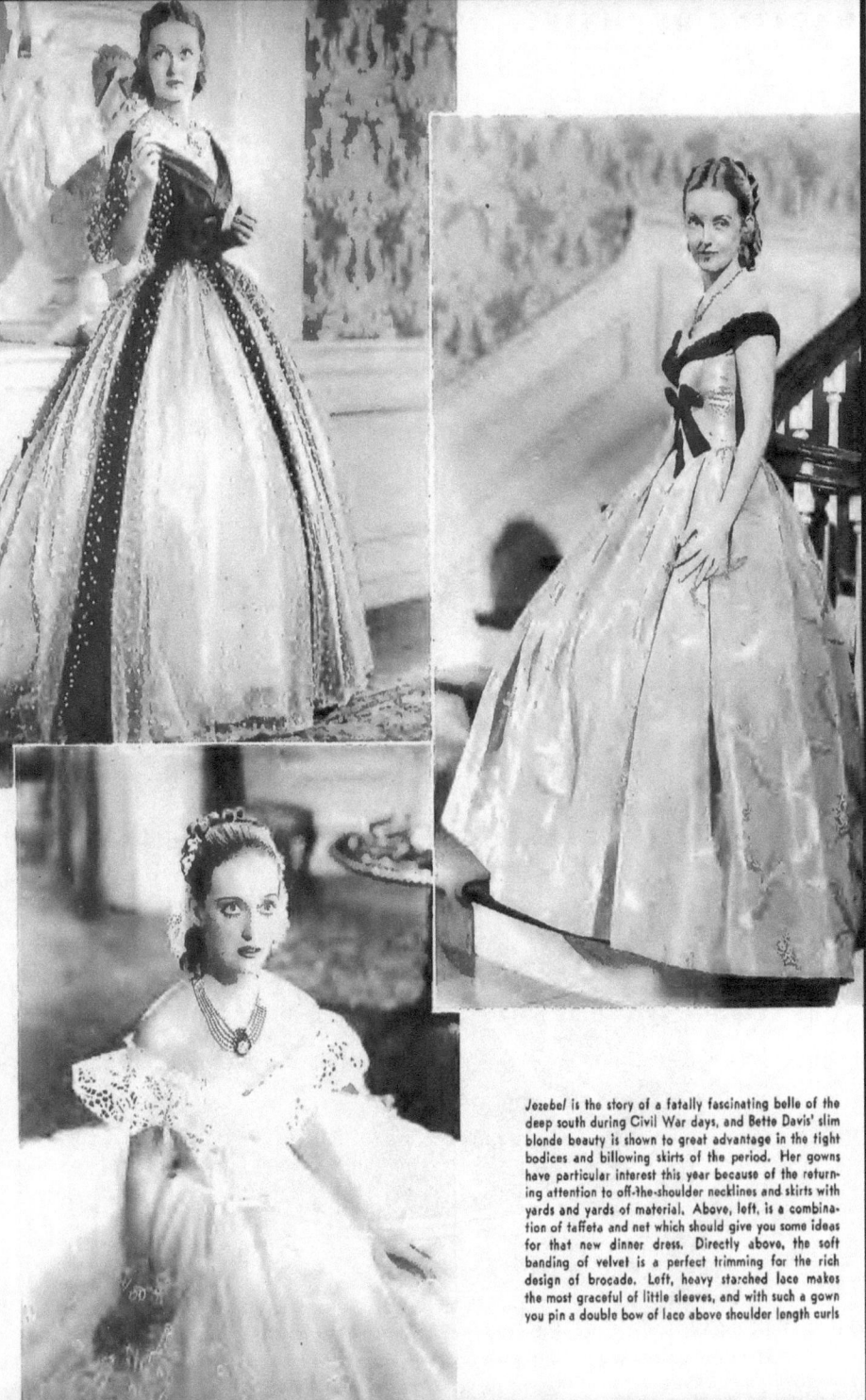

Jezebel is the story of a fatally fascinating belle of the deep south during Civil War days, and Bette Davis' slim blonde beauty is shown to great advantage in the tight bodices and billowing skirts of the period. Her gowns have particular interest this year because of the returning attention to off-the-shoulder necklines and skirts with yards and yards of material. Above, left, is a combination of taffeta and net which should give you some ideas for that new dinner dress. Directly above, the soft banding of velvet is a perfect trimming for the rich design of brocade. Left, heavy starched lace makes the most graceful of little sleeves, and with such a gown you pin a double bow of lace above shoulder length curls

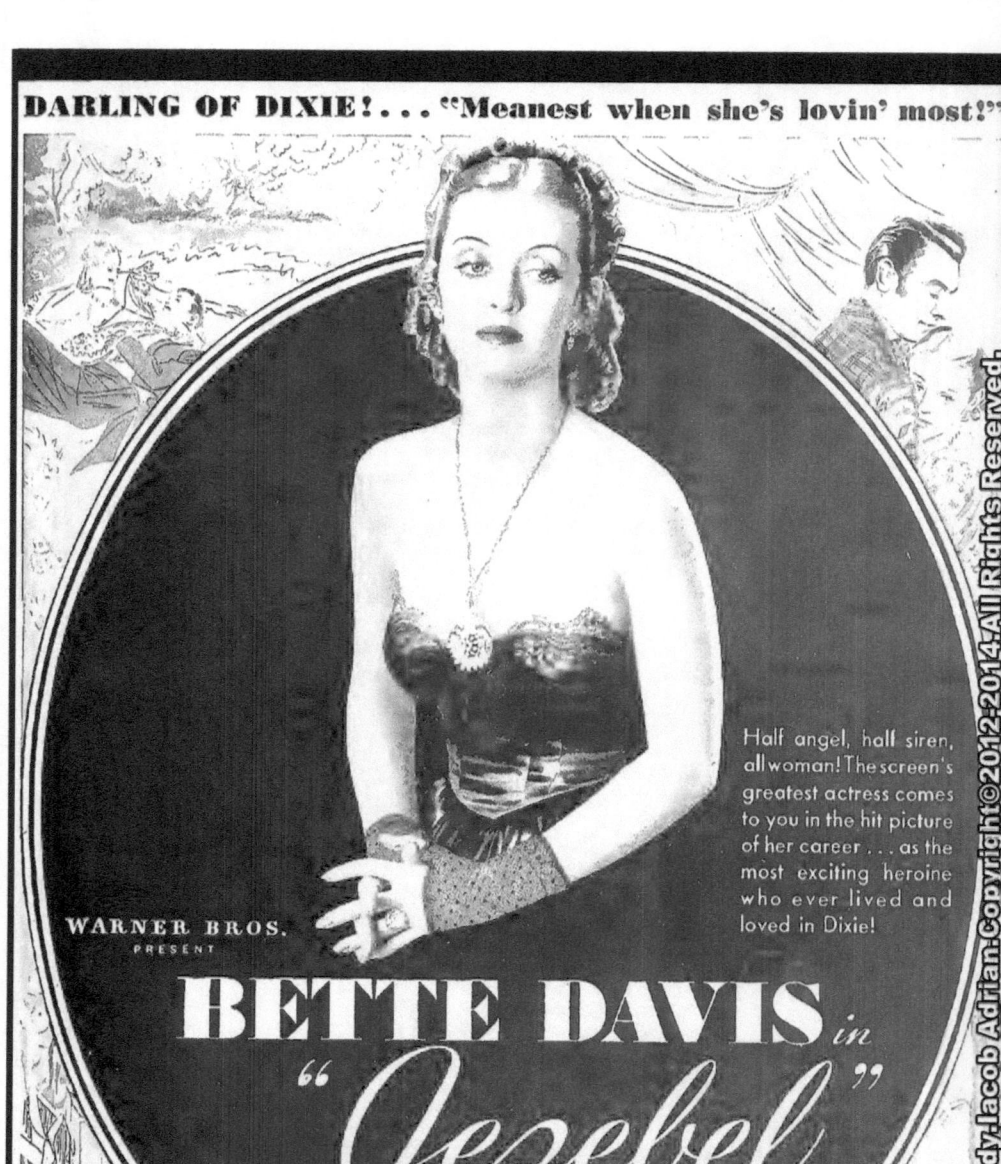

DARLING OF DIXIE!... **"Meanest when she's lovin' most!"**

Half angel, half siren, all woman! The screen's greatest actress comes to you in the hit picture of her career ... as the most exciting heroine who ever lived and loved in Dixie!

WARNER BROS.
PRESENT

BETTE DAVIS *in*

"Jezebel"

THE GREATEST ROMANCE
OF THE SOUTH

HENRY FONDA · GEORGE BRENT · Margaret Lindsay · Donald Crisp · Fay Bainter
RICHARD CROMWELL · HENRY O'NEILL · SPRING BYINGTON · JOHN LITEL

Screen Play by Clements Ripley,
Abem Finkel and John Huston

A WILLIAM WYLER PRODUCTION

From the Play by Owen Davis, Sr.
Music by Max Steiner

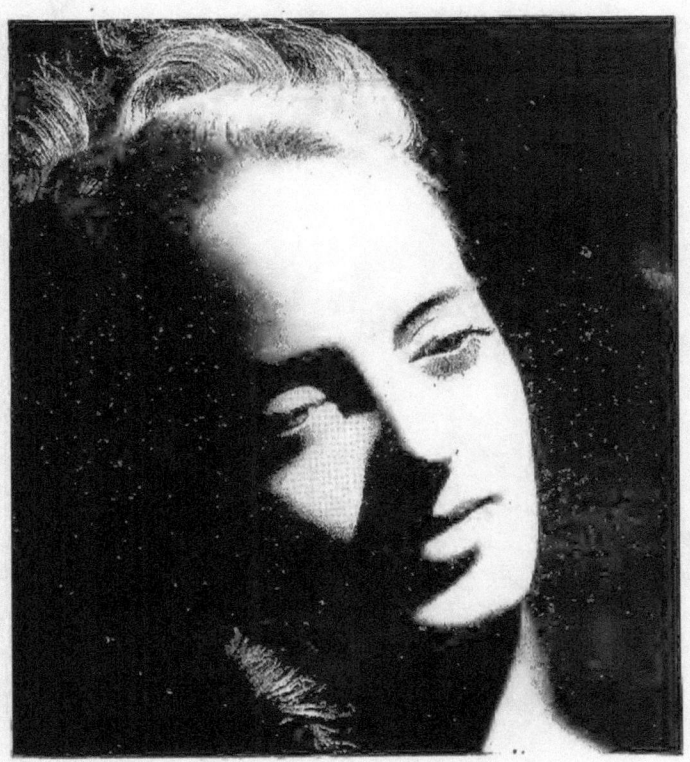

STUDY THIS FACE!

You'll never forget it. For here are forever written the ecstasy and pain of woman loved and loving. Here is the face of Bette Davis in her supreme dramatic triumph, "Dark Victory." Here is the screen's most gifted actress in a role which is destined to win for her another Academy Award. Watch for "Dark Victory"—a Warner Bros. presentation—in America's leading theatres soon.

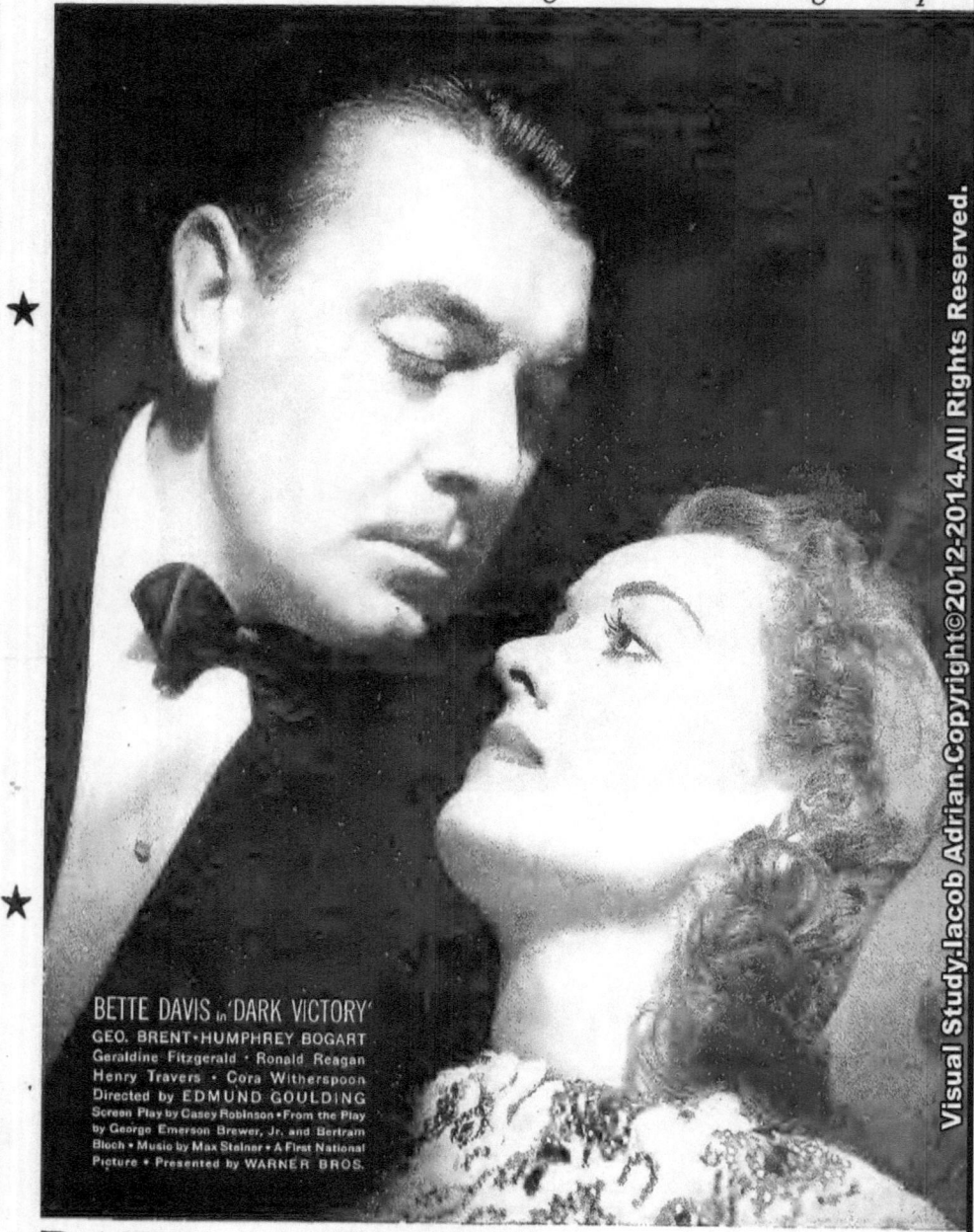

★ **BETTE DAVIS** *Brings You Her Crowning Triumph!*

BETTE DAVIS in 'DARK VICTORY'
GEO. BRENT • HUMPHREY BOGART
Geraldine Fitzgerald • Ronald Reagan
Henry Travers • Cora Witherspoon
Directed by EDMUND GOULDING
Screen Play by Casey Robinson • From the Play
by George Emerson Brewer, Jr. and Bertram
Bloch • Music by Max Steiner • A First National
Picture • Presented by WARNER BROS.

★ **DARK VICTORY** Never a story of love so exquisite!…She smiled at the cost, and bravely paid the reckoning when her heart's happy dancing was ended.

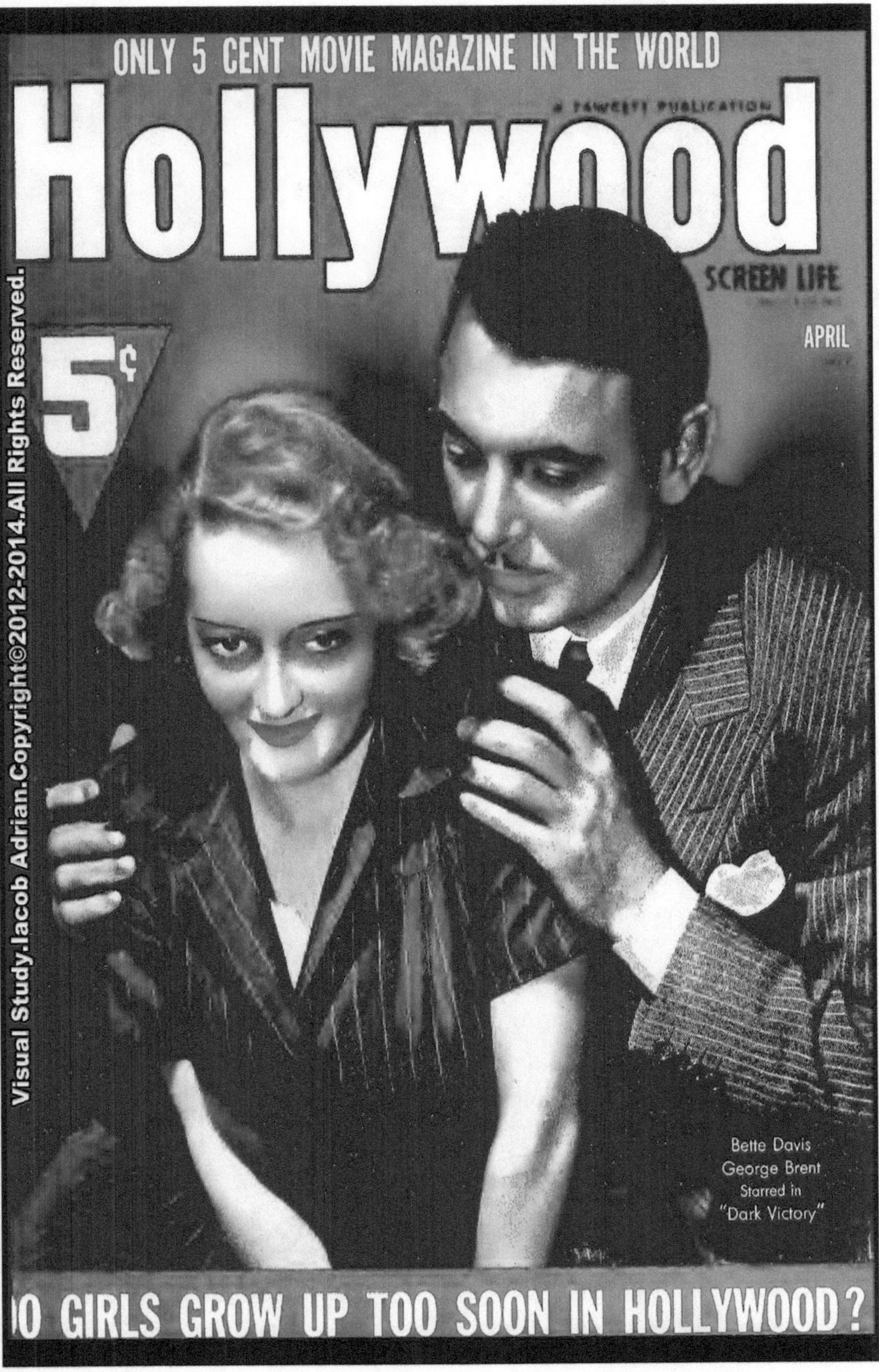

Hollywood

A FAWCETT PUBLICATION

SCREEN LIFE

APRIL

5¢

Bette Davis
George Brent
Starred in
"Dark Victory"

DO GIRLS GROW UP TOO SOON IN HOLLYWOOD?

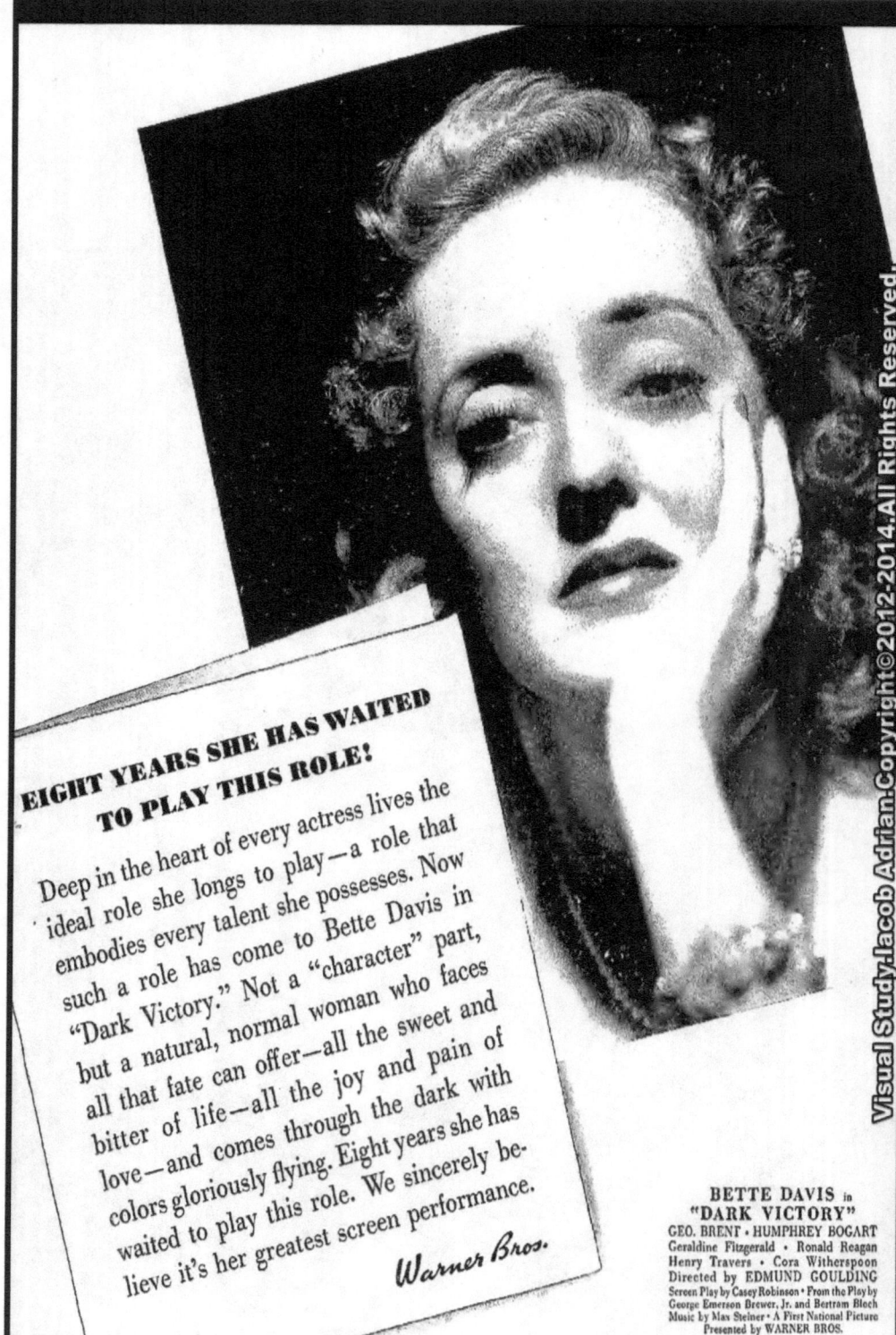

EIGHT YEARS SHE HAS WAITED TO PLAY THIS ROLE!

Deep in the heart of every actress lives the ideal role she longs to play—a role that embodies every talent she possesses. Now such a role has come to Bette Davis in "Dark Victory." Not a "character" part, but a natural, normal woman who faces all that fate can offer—all the sweet and bitter of life—all the joy and pain of love—and comes through the dark with colors gloriously flying. Eight years she has waited to play this role. We sincerely be-lieve it's her greatest screen performance.

Warner Bros.

BETTE DAVIS in
"DARK VICTORY"
GEO. BRENT • HUMPHREY BOGART
Geraldine Fitzgerald • Ronald Reagan
Henry Travers • Cora Witherspoon
Directed by EDMUND GOULDING
Screen Play by Casey Robinson • From the Play by
George Emerson Brewer, Jr. and Bertram Bloch
Music by Max Steiner • A First National Picture
Presented by WARNER BROS.

The Portrait of a Free Soul

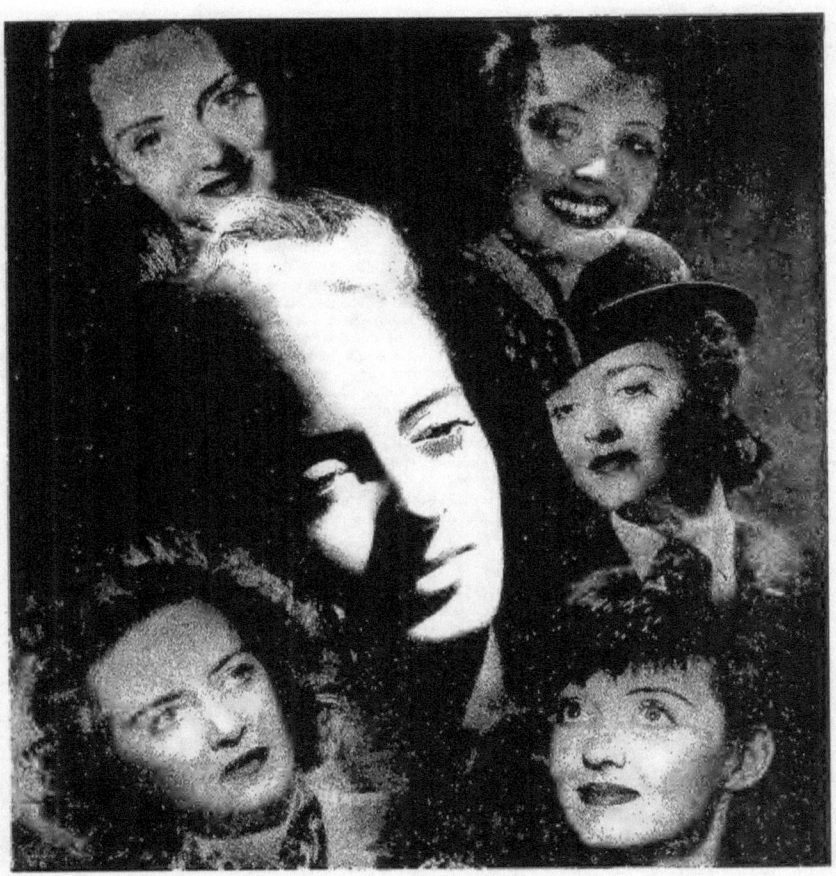

NOW SEE THIS FACE ON THE SCREEN!

Out of the blazing fires of her genius, the screen's most gifted actress has created a gallery of unforgettable women. Now Bette Davis, the winner of two Academy Awards, comes to you in the climax of all her dramatic triumphs. In the role she has waited eight years to play. In the greatest picture of a woman's love that the world has yet seen. See "Dark Victory," a Warner Bros. picture, at your theatre Easter Week!

Juarez Highlights

■ Empress Bette Davis—oh, well, then, Empress Carlotta of Mexico—was wandering around between scenes on the *Juarez* throne-room set. Below a remarkably becoming coal black wig, Bette's clear skin and small features had a cameo quality. She really did look like Winterhalter portraits of Carlotta. Her gown—

"Miss Davis! Hey! Hey, Bette! Wait a second! Hold it!"

Two electricians yelled at her simultaneously, with such vigor that Director William Dieterle jumped, and the heads of the camera crew jerked about as if on swivels. Astonished, Bette halted. They waved her away with frantic shooing motions. As her brocaded slippers hesitantly retreated, one of the men gasped: "That dress! ZOW-ie!"

Bette had been about to step across a snarl of electric cables and connection boxes. And the billowy hoop skirts of her

Sit in on the filming of one of the biggest pictures of the new season

By

SERENA BRADFORD

court gown were heavily embroidered with $1,200 worth of gold, silver and copper—they were so stiff with metal that they practically stood alone—and if those burnished folds brushed a defective bit of wiring, the result might have been electrocution. Warner Brothers decided to take no chances. Until the scene had been filmed and the gown put away, a prop boy was detailed to follow Bette, murmuring, "Watch it!" at the proper moments.

"Heavens," Bette commented, "a nice outfit to wear in a thunderstorm, eh?"

The real Carlotta, who lived till 1927, ran no risk from electric wires'

in the three years, when, with Emperor Maximilian, she ruled over Mexico. When their rule began in the spring of 1864, the palace outside Mexico City at Chapultepec was lighted by candles in great golden candelabra. Replicas of them appear in the adoption scene for which Bette had donned the gorgeous metal dress.

To understand the whys and wherefores of the scene, shall we take a quick blink at history? It beats the wildest melodrama, this time.

A Belgian princess who became an Austrian Archduchess (by marriage) at twenty, an Empress at twenty-four, and a hopeless madwoman at twenty-eight; this sums up the career of Carlotta. As for Maximilian (Brian Aherne),·he was an honorable man who thought he had been freely chosen by the Mexicans as their Emperor. But soon he discovered that he was merely a puppet of the French monarch; and that the Mexicans preferred their Indian patriot, Juarez, who had recently declared Mexico a Republic with himself as President.

For the rest: At the end of the Civil

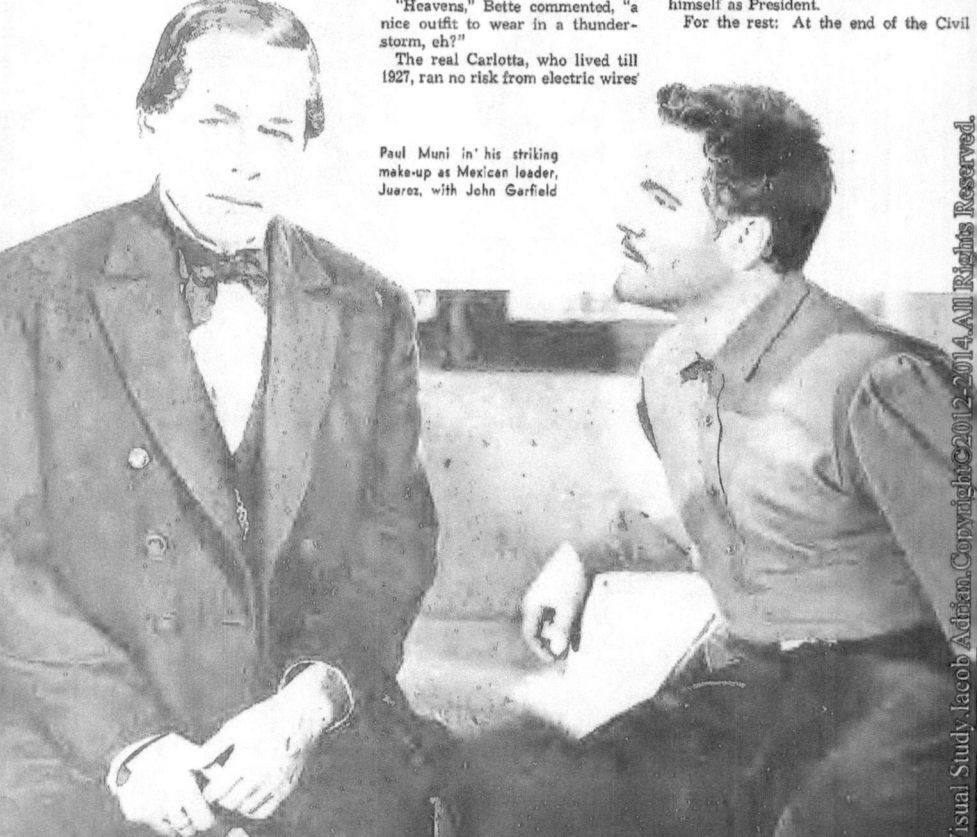

Paul Muni in' his striking make-up as Mexican leader, Juarez, with John Garfield

War, the United States frowned upon a foreign emperor in America, and extended aid to Juarez. France then withdrew from Maximilian her troops and support. Carlotta, rushing to Europe, vainly begged help for the husband whom she devotedly loved. When news came of Maximilian's death before a Juarez firing squad, Carlotta's reason snapped. She spent the rest of her long life, closely guarded, in a Belgian castle. To the end, she believed herself still to be Empress of Mexico.

◼ The high peak of magnificence for both Carlotta and Maximilian was the day of their adoption of an heir. Maximilian, still ruler, needed a son to consolidate the empire which he had accepted (against the advice of his elder brother, Franz Joseph of Austria) from Louis Napoleon.

Amid the splendor of the Chapultepec throne room, the imperial couple sat in their chairs of state, their ermine robes trailing down the steps of the dais. At the foot of the steps stood a small boy in black velvet suit and royal robe, looking small indeed against the enormous room with its crowd of court ladies and officers, diplomats and clerics. Augustin Iturbide, orphan of an aristocratic Mexican family, was to take the place of the son who had been denied to the Emperor and Empress, despite Carlotta's agonized prayers. With solemn rites the officials pronounced this child the heir and successor of Maximilian, little knowing how soon and how hurriedly they would send the lad north to the political safety of the United States.

The adoption scene over (there were real tears in Bette's eyes and probably there had been in poor Carlotta's, too), the company moved to another set for an earlier episode in the film: the arrival of the Emperor and Empress at Vera Cruz. For this sequence, part of the Vera Cruz waterfront had been reproduced; a square-rigged ship chartered; an arch of triumph erected. Quaint sights greeted the Empress, quaint and foreign after the sedate elegance of the marble

Right, one of the most colorful periods of Mexican history was the short reign of the lovely Carlotta (Bette Davis) and the tragic Maximilian (Brian Aherne)

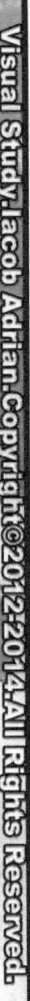

Below, little Mickey Kuhn kneels before Brian Aherne and Bette Davis during the impressive adoption scene

Below, Claude Rains, as Napoleon, discusses problems of empire with the Empress Eugenie (Gale Sondergaard)

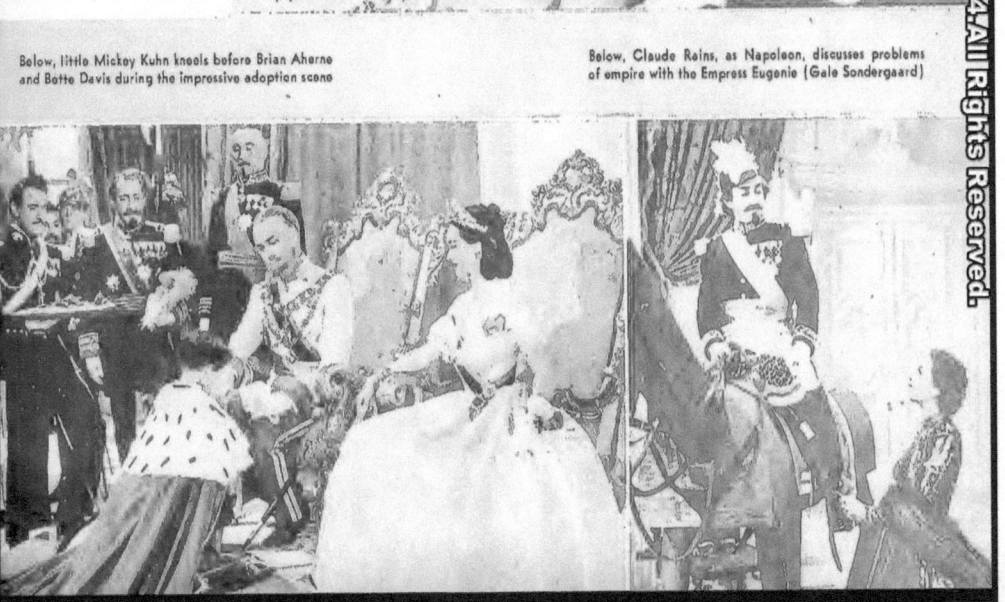

Juarez Highlights

palace on the Adriatic Sea where she and her youthful husband had been so happy.

A profusion of exotic flowers, an outburst of cheers—but nobody except soldiers were on the twisted white streets, and there were so many vultures! Maximilian began to wonder uneasily. They didn't tell him that numberless executions had taken care of those who conspicuously objected to his coming. Bette, in her high-necked, puffed-sleeved blue gown, the color of the ocean, climbed into the imperial coach, a marvel of black enamel and gold leaf. On the cushions was a paper. It was a message from Juarez: "You are the victim of a fraud, designed to make you believe that the people of Mexico desire an Emperor. I tell you to leave Mexico and never return . . ."

Maximilian could not believe that this paper told the truth. In the role of the ruler, Brian Aherne looked at it first with uneasiness, then with a half smile, while his retinue scoffed at the Indian upstart who ventured such a warning. The great Emperor had no way of knowing how important the poor peon was to be.

What about the "Indian upstart," Juarez, as played by Paul Muni?

History records that he was outwardly calm, even exasperatingly unhurried. He handled documents with clumsy, slow fingers. His brain seemed to plod. But that's what deceived the people of his own era, at first. Behind that dogged exterior was an unbreakable will and the mind of a keen and adroit soldier. His usual stolidity made his few flashes of fire the more effective.

The "village" which housed the Juarez headquarters stood as a triumph of the movie technicians' skill. Built at the Warner ranch in San Fernando Valley, it was designed largely from plaster casts of the walls of local Spanish missions. The casts picked up the impressions of weather markings, water furrows, and sand erosions found on the ancient stone and adobe structures, and these markings were transferred to the buildings in the outdoor sets.

Consequently, three strides across a patch of grass, you found yourself in the middle of old Mexico. There stood a cathedral at one end of a steep street, its chunky tower sharp against the sapphire sky; a cathedral complete with weather-beaten gray portico and crumbling steps. Farther on was an inn with hospitable doorway and iron-grilled windows. At the brow of the hill stood some houses with purple vines over the lower porches and a lop-eared balcony or two upstairs. Casement windows swung in the wind. Curtains flapped. The chipped house cornices, the powdery pink stone of the fountain, the streaks and stains and cracks on the walls of shops . . Why, the place looked as if it had been there five centuries.

■ It's a pity they couldn't have had in the picture one Luis Flores Lopez, who lives in Mexico City and who has attained the mature age of 116 years. Lopez, who fought under Juarez's aide, Porfirio Diaz, throughout the time Maximilian was Emperor, acted as technical adviser on the film, and gave Director Dieterle many valuable suggestions when Dieterle went to Mexico for data.

One of Lopez's deeds of derring-do has been duplicated in the picture. During an engagement with the French artillery, he rode up to the gun emplacement, unarmed, lassoed a field piece, and dragged it back to the Mexican lines. This act of courage was witnessed by Col. Gabriel Moreno, now aged 90; and by General Ignacio Velasquez, now 108 years old, who was the commanding officer during that engagement. Apparently one way to live long is to join a Mexican revolution.

And it looked for a while as if the way to have a short life was to join the cast of *Juarez*. Gilbert Roland, who plays the role of a Mexican officer, averted two bad accidents in as many days. First he saved the $20,000 royal coach and doubtless the life of Bette's stand-in when he stopped a bad runaway by spurring his horse forward and seizing a bridle. The next day— still doing things not in the script—he saved Bette from almost certain injury by

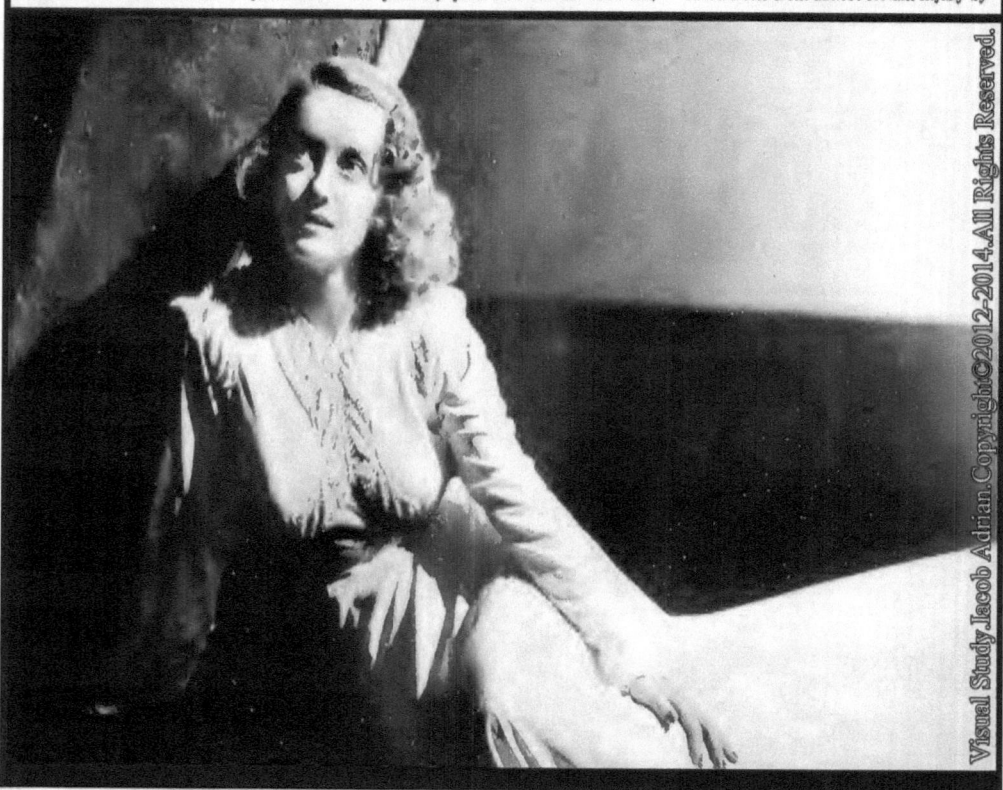

throwing his mount off balance and to the ground after it had suddenly reared and seemed about to plunge into Bette's lap.

Great pains have been taken to give the film authenticity. Many objects were brought from Mexico, and a $50,000 shipload of authentic Louis Napoleon art objects is part of the "atmosphere." The wardrobe furnished 3,000 outfits; the property department 10,000 "props;" the make-up department $2,500 worth of whiskers. Maximilian's four beards cost $500, and the rest of the cast used five hundred whisker items from "the works," to the tiny patch that John Garfield, as Porfirio Diaz, wore on his chin.

Even the stars in the skies are correctly placed. Director Dieterle is a believer in horoscopes, so he had somebody work out the exact position in which the stars were on the evening of the famous "adoption day." So the constellations you see twinkling beyond the windows of Chapultepec palace when that day ends are the same as those which Carlotta and Maximilian saw. Thus, to his own satisfaction, Dieterle combined both astronomy and astrology. He felt that the ill-starred royal pair were entitled, in his picture, anyway, to the stars to which they were accustomed.

Perhaps because the theme is so tragic, Juarez handed the cast more unplanned laughs in the course of production than you'll find (more's the pity) in many a comedy. Paul Muni tried one little scene seven times before he got through it without interruption. Tiny upsets ruined the first three takes; in Take 4, a fly landed on Muni's nose; Take 5, an airplane droned above the sound stage; Take 6, the mikes picked up a long peal of thunder which turned out to be the rolling of an embarrassed actor's tummy.

Quite a lot of the merriment centered around the flaring hoop skirts of Carlotta. Once, at a lakeside, a breeze caught those hoops and Bette, finding them as unmanageable as balloons, had to be saved from taking flight by a corps of cameramen. And in the big scene when Carlotta's mind feels its first touch of insanity, those hoops got in their work again.

Prince Metternich, the Austrian Ambassador, had called. "Your Imperial Majesty," he began.

Bette whirled about to face him. Her foot caught in the folds, the heavy hoops swung, and Her Imperial Majesty went flat on the floor. She might have been *really* mad that time, but once more she laughed. For a film Empress, there's nothing like a sense of humor.

It doesn't hurt for an Emperor to have a sense of humor, either. After a nice picnic lunch out at the ranch, Brian Aherne learned that he was to face the firing squad. All afternoon. So, for fun, he took a quick look at the calls for next day to see what the future had in store. His call read: "Brian Aherne. Stage 7. 9 a.m. Interior coffin."

Aherne shrugged. "Oh, well," he said, "that's life in the movies."

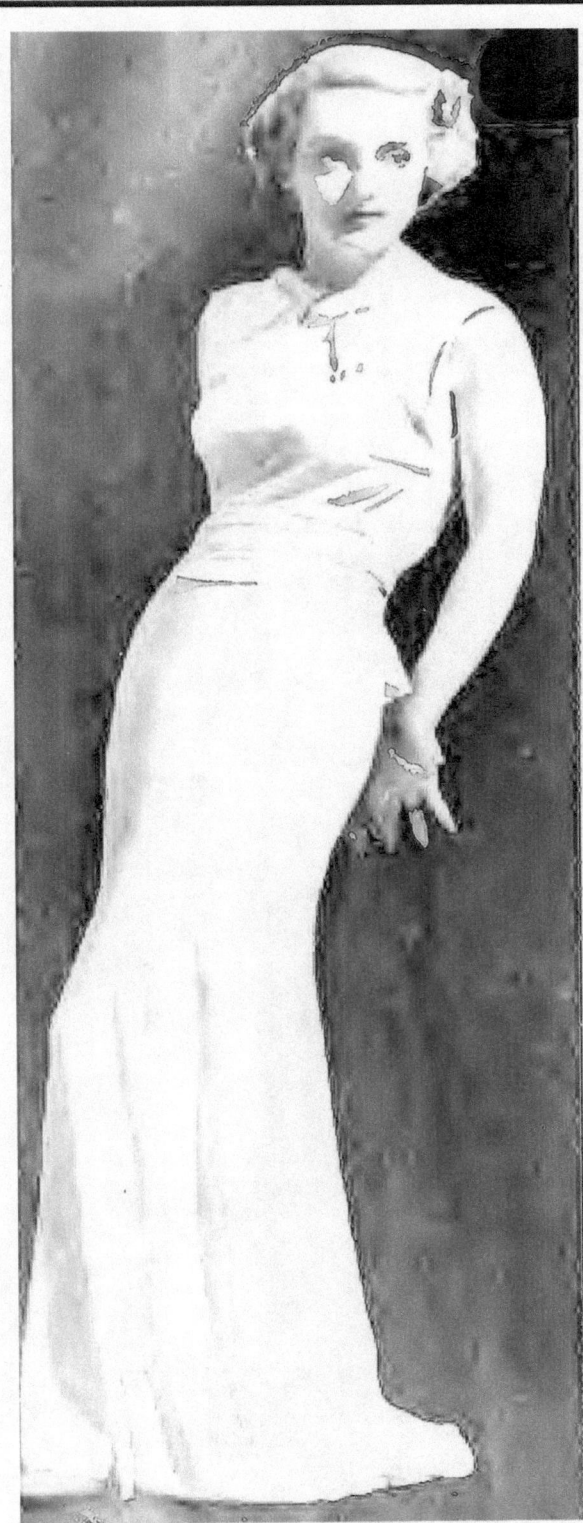

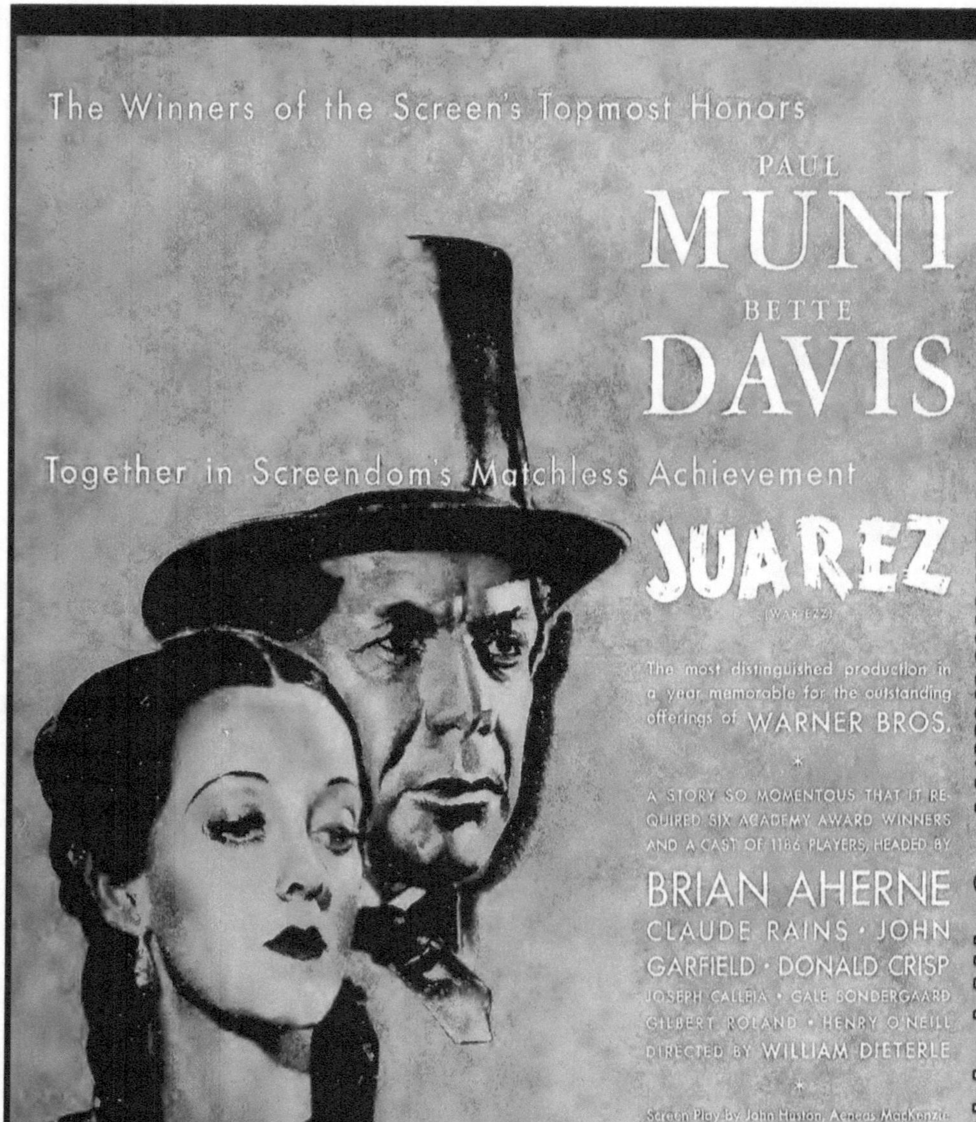

The Winners of the Screen's Topmost Honors

PAUL
MUNI
BETTE
DAVIS

Together in Screendom's Matchless Achievement

JUAREZ
(WAR-EZZ)

The most distinguished production in a year memorable for the outstanding offerings of WARNER BROS.

*

A STORY SO MOMENTOUS THAT IT REQUIRED SIX ACADEMY AWARD WINNERS AND A CAST OF 1186 PLAYERS, HEADED BY

BRIAN AHERNE
CLAUDE RAINS · JOHN GARFIELD · DONALD CRISP
JOSEPH CALLEIA · GALE SONDERGAARD
GILBERT ROLAND · HENRY O'NEILL
DIRECTED BY WILLIAM DIETERLE

*

Screen Play By John Huston, Aeneas MacKenzie and Wolfgang Reinhardt. Based on a Play by Franz Werfel and the Novel, "The Phantom Crown," by Bertita Harding. Music by Erich Wolfgang Korngold

SEE IT! YOU'LL NEVER FORGET IT!

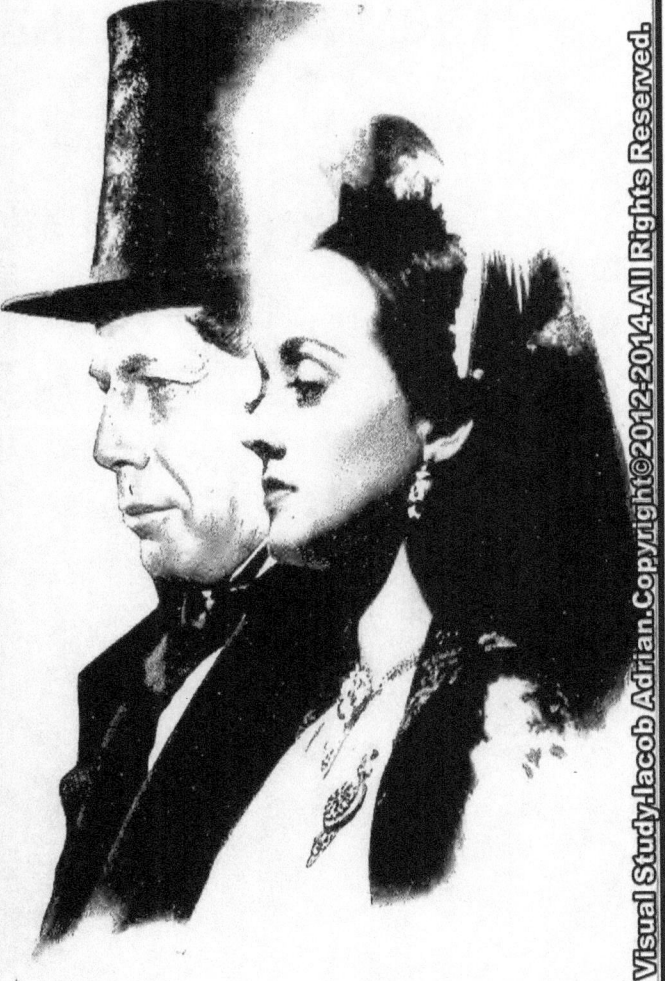

Announcing

THE PICTURE
MAGNIFICENT!

The story of Juarez, Mexican flame of freedom . . . moulding a fiery-hearted people into a nation that toppled a throne! . . . The story of Carlota, empress to Maximilian . . . burning her fateful romance into the pages of history! . . . All in a glorious human drama sweeping through scenes never matched in action, splendor and power! See "Juarez" at your theatre soon! The picture that shows how great the screen can be!

WARNER BROS. PRESENT

PAUL MUNI · BETTE DAVIS
in
"JUAREZ"
with
BRIAN AHERNE
CLAUDE RAINS · JOHN GARFIELD · DONALD CRISP
JOSEPH CALLEIA · GALE SONDERGAARD · GILBERT ROLAND · HENRY O'NEILL

Directed by William Dieterle

Screen Play by John Huston, Aeneas MacKenzie and Wolfgang Reinhardt • Based on a Play by Franz Werfel and the Novel, "The Phantom Crown," by Bertita Harding • Music by Erich Wolfgang Korngold

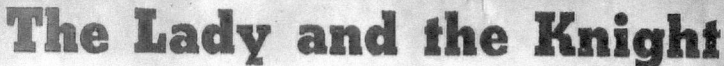

The Lady and the Knight

BY JESSIE HENDERSON

Bette Davis, in heavy make-up, as the 45-year-old Elizabeth, fights her love for ambitious young, dashing, obstinate Essex who is played by Errol Flynn

Take a trip backstage and watch the filming of the tragic story of the love of Elizabeth and head-strong Essex

It had been a pretty tough day for the Queen. The courtiers were a-muttering in Whitehall Palace corners against her sweetheart, handsome young Essex. The Irish rebels were on the rampage. Essex was looking sidewise at a dark-eyed lady-in-waiting. And the royal flame-colored velvet robes, studded in diamonds, gold and topaz, weighed 97 pounds as against Queen Elizabeth's own weight of 110 . . . with the temperature under the lights on Stage 9 at 120 degrees.

Yes, a tough day, and bound to grow tougher. For *now* they wanted her to break mirrors! "It isn't bad luck if you do it on purpose," they soothed.

"Whoof!" ejaculated good Queen Bette Davis, dropping into her great canvas chair before the empty fireplace in the "Queen's Closet." The

44

chair, placed there temporarily to catch the Queen before she sank under the weight of her velvet splendor, was especially constructed by Warner Brothers' prop department to accommodate the wideflung regal skirts.

Somebody opened the sound stage doors. Hot sunlight and a wisp of sultry breeze poured into the stone walled "Closet"—a parlor, really—with its high, narrow, stained glass windows decked out in armorial shields. "Whoof!" said the Queen again.

"Cigarette?" asked Sir Walter Raleigh —as well he might. It was Raleigh, you remember, who first brought tobacco to England from the colony of Virginia, which had been named for the Virgin Queen. Good Queen Bess tried a pipeful of it once, and pronounced the stuff not bad. Good Queen Bette got out a 12-inch paper holder and carefully put into it the cigarette which towering Sir Walter (Vincent Price, 6 ft. 4½ ins., from the New York stage) offered from his pack. She looked anxiously after her gigantic lace ruff while he gave her a light.

"Anybody wants to be queen," she remarked to Tibbie, the pet Scottie, "can have it." Bette ought to know her own mind on that subject; she's lately been the Empress Carlotta, too. Tibbie gave a feeble flick of the tail in reply. Since Bette had donned that red Elizabeth wig, Tibbie wouldn't come out from under the dressing table. Before they toned the wig down and tamed its curls to royal dignity for technicolor camera requirements, Bette, herself, said she looked like Harpo Marx.

She didn't look like Harpo on the day I saw her. She looked like a weary woman of 45 trying to appear girlish, without benefit of beauty salons, for a lover of 25 —and she'd had the dickens of an argument with the makeup department in order to achieve that appearance.

They wanted to glamourize her. "What!" cried Bette with vehemence — for she knows her history—"*glamour*! For Elizabeth! In those days, she was absolutely a hag, and I'm going to look like a hag or I won't play the role!" She added: "Why, the whole point of the plot is Elizabeth's fear that a youth couldn't love her, and the fact that the youth doesn't."

So Bette plucked her eyebrows (Elizabeth's were very thin), and shaved her forehead hairline (because Elizabeth's hair grew scant), and had them do things to her face in the matter of wrinkles and pouches which very few Hollywood stars would have permitted, much less insisted upon.

So, she looked like Elizabeth at 45 or better, fading, but still vain; jealous, anxious, suspicious, eager to be reassured; a great Queen and a proud woman, able to give her hot-headed young lover every splendid gift he craved, except the gift of youth to match his youth..... Why, Bette had wanted to play one scene without the wig, practically bald! She wanted to play *Elizabeth*—not a glamour tootsie.

"What's Essex up to *now*?" demanded Bette, glancing toward a corner of the stage whence arose hoots of merriment. Essex (Errol Flynn) in crimson velvet doublet and hose, slashed with gold, his

gold-fretted steel corselet and helmet laid aside for the moment, had thrown back his head (he wears in this picture a truly distinguished, small Vandyke beard) and, shaken with suppressed laughter, was holding to the shoulder of Sir Francis Bacon (Donald Crisp) for support. (They had lots of gags about "Crisp Bacon.")

The Queen scooped up her farthingale and petticoat, and went to investigate. When she reached the corner, Olivia de Havilland (she has the role of Lady Penelope Gray, the Queen's rival in the affections of Essex) was peering through a magnifying glass at a tapestry, rich in dim reds and greens, purples and blues, which hung upon the wall of the Throne Room.

"I don't see anything," Olivia said unsuspectingly.

"Here, let me fix the glass," Flynn offered. He touched a spring and Olivia leaped into the air with shock and surprise. A squirt of water had hit her square in the face.

"I might have known!" she said, stamping a foot in pretended wrath, as a makeup man stepped forward with tissue to mop her dry.

"Kid stuff, by my halidome," remarked the Queen, and at once matched it. From somewhere in her voluminous attire she produced Lily. Lily is a mechanical sheep which sings the song about Mary's little lamb. Bette wound up Lily and put her on the floor, to the mingled astonishment and concern of Flynn's huge schnauzer, Arno.

Arno, whom they once found asleep on the $1200 hand carving and $800 velours cushions of the Queen's throne, couldn't abide Lily. But just as, goggle-eyed, he extended a devastating paw. Director Michael Curtiz called out in his Hungarian English: "Everybody get closer together apart, please. We go!"

So the camera crew got closer together apart. Bette sat in her chair of State. Essex knelt at her feet. It was THE love scene.

Olivia de Havilland plays Lady Penelope whose beauty and sharp tongue make her a dangerous rival to the aging Queen

Fifteen minutes of it, rehearsed for a week —the key scene of the picture.

Essex, the darling of Elizabeth and of the populace, won glory in the Spanish war but quarreled with the Queen after his return. This was their reconciliation. Not long afterward, he failed as conqueror of the Irish rebels (a fine thing, sending a man named Flynn to fight against the Irish), and hurried back to London to appease Elizabeth. Here he made a fatal error. He raised a company of followers, marched on the palace, and tried to abduct the Queen.

Hurt to the quick by this treason of her lover, Elizabeth imprisoned him in the Tower of London and sentenced him to the block. At the last moment—according to the Maxwell Anderson stage play, "Elizabeth the Queen," from which the film is taken, but not according to history—Elizabeth summoned Essex to a room in the Tower, begged him to marry her. But (again in the film, not in history) Essex chose the block because he knew that, given the chance, he would try to seize the crown for himself, alone. This, briefly, is the story of Elizabeth's tragic romance in her later years.

"We go!" said Curtiz ... The love scene started well with Essex romantic and melting, Elizabeth tender. Then, in a rush of emotion, the Queen threw her arms about the knight's neck and pulled him toward her. Flynn, upon one knee, lost his balance and completely folded up; simply fell kerplunk across the royal lap. Dignity fled.

The Queen howled. Essex slid to the floor and sat there, chortling. The voice of Curtiz rose above the general mirth: "Bette, I guess you don't know your own strength, isn't it?"

The scene was resumed and this time it went through unmarred to its end; fervent, pathetic, stirring. It is one of the most remarkable and touching love scenes ever put upon celluloid. Elizabeth was ruthless, as perhaps a monarch had to be, but in that sequence Bette leaves you weak with sympathy for a lonely, hard old woman who, in agony of soul, tried to capture the one thing the world had never given her: genuine love.

When the scene was ended, the Queen's Grace nibbled at an ice cream cone with due regard to precious farthingale and stomacher, and Lord Burghley (Henry Stephenson) took a swig from a bottle of pop without spilling it down his velvet and brocade doublet. Both watched the prop boys setting up mirrors in the Queen's boudoir. Bette eyed them askance. She's superstitious.

The panelled boudoir and all the other rooms in Whitehall Palace, were reproduced at much cost from drawings made in London. Whitehall as it stands now— Government offices have occupied it these many hundred years—is only a building erected upon the site of the original palace, which was burned in 1689. Recently, however, the British Government excavated the foundations and what is left of the original walls, and the Warners' set was carefully based on authentic data. Its dark carved panels, its sombre stone, its arched fireplaces, form a perfect techni-

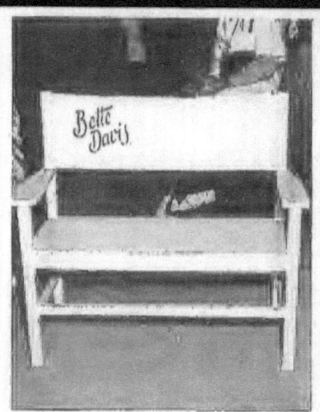

Especially built to accommodate the heavy spreading skirts of Queen Elizabeth's costumes was this chair, used on the set by Bette Davis between scenes

color background for the rich costumes of the court.

The Tudor times were noted for extravagantly beautiful dress. And the Queen led them all. On State occasions she even commanded her maids of honor to wear white so that her own robes would shine forth with the more magnificence.

When Essex gives a little hawking party at his country place in Wanstead, Bette wears a bottle green brocade riding habit with a long green velvet cloak. Once, at the Council table, she wears white quilted satin sewn all over with pearls. For the love scene she has a changeable green and bronze taffeta, with a high, delicate lace ruff. The dress is embroidered in gold and emeralds. A pendant of rubies, diamonds, and pearls is at her throat, pearl drops are in her ears, and on her fingers sparkle five rings of rubies, pearls, diamonds, emeralds, and aquamarines.

As for the men—the Warner's wardrobe department order for a man's costume was usually so many yards of velvet and six pounds of sawdust. It seems the Elizabethans achieved that swank baggy-knee breeches effect by the aid of a lumber yard. Flynn is thoroughly well dressed as Essex. He wears beige suede, black velvet and gold trimmings under his armor in Ireland. Dark green velvet with silver braid, and blue-green brocatelle edged with silver make a Court costume.

■ But Bette's mind was not on the subject of dress at the moment. She was looking at those mirrors, just put up around the royal boudoir wall. "You're sure it's okay to break them if you do it on purpose?" she inquired again.

There had been (some days before, in accordance with the jigsaw Hollywood custom) a savage scene between Elizabeth and Lady Penelope Gray which Bette was to play the climax of it. Lady Penelope, intrepid wench! had responded surprisingly to the Queen's order to take her lute in hand and sing a song.

Instead of the real verses of "The Passionate Shepherd"—a ballad popular in Elizabeth's day—Penelope sang some verses lately improvised by the Queen's ex-favorite, Raleigh. Far in the past was the chivalrous cloak-and-puddle incident whereby Raleigh had won favor with Elizabeth, and Raleigh was envious of the current power of Essex. His verses, therefore, deftly and subtly twitted the Queen on her fading charms. By contrast, as she sang them, Penelope's fresh loveliness stood out radiantly.

You know Elizabeth's red-headed temper? Only that fortnight, in the throne room, Essex had ventured to contradict her. Smack! Right before the entire Court her hand shot out and caught Essex down the side of the face and the mouth. And this was Essex, mind you ... the man Elizabeth loved.

Accordingly, when Penelope sang the jeering verses, nobody would have been surprised if royal assault and battery, perhaps even the headsman's axe, had resulted. But Elizabeth, woman as well as Queen, realized how the Court would buzz if she dignified the incident by too much notice. She dismissed her ladies with the air of a cobra ready to spring and, when the door closed, walked up to a mirror.

Fading charms! True. With new eyes she studied her drawn features, the wrinkled forehead, the lines around the mouth. And then Elizabeth (despite Bette's superstitious qualms) picked up a vase and crashed it into the glass. Tankards, chairs, whatever weapon came handy, she hurled at the other mirrors in the room. It turned out that Bette's aim was equally bad with either hand. She broke 28 mirrors before she was able to go through the scene and plant a direct hit on each glass in turn. "Anybody should have a wife couldn't aim any better," Curtiz gaily commented.

■ Alas for those who said breaking mirrors a-purpose didn't count! Superstition or not, here's what happened. Olivia was laid up 24 hours when she banged her leg against a heavy table. Bette stayed home ten days with laryngitis. And Flynn delayed production a week when an accident required four stitches in his eyelid.

It's a wonder, though, that half the cast didn't come from the picture with web feet, considering the length of time Essex and his men spent in that Irish bog on Stage 11! It was a two and one-half acre bog, complete with trees and hummocks and water and stumps and a thick Irish fog that drifted in whenever Curtiz ordered it. Through this bog, Essex chased Tyrone, the Irish rebel leader (Alan Hale).

Technicolor requires more lights than ordinary film. Thanks to the lights, the temperature on the set, even upon cool days, was (take a deep breath and reach for a fan) 127.

■ But temperature and wet weren't the only things that bothered the English troops and the Irish rebels who played hide and seek among the misty tree trunks. On a Monday the cast assembled in the bog to discover that during the week end

it had been taken over by frogs from the adjacent Los Angeles river. The hoarse, delighted croaks (for there was more water on the sound stage than in the riverbed at that season) almost drowned the Curtiz thunderings.

"Get those froggies out!" he shouted, "somebody ribs me, no?"

With nets from the prop department, the cast spent an hilarious hour capturing the froggies and sending them back to the river—by special messenger.

It was while Essex fought rebels and froggies that the Queen fumed because she had no word from him. . . . She did not guess that Raleigh and Lady Penelope intercepted his letters.

But Elizabeth was shrewd and she did suspect the Lady Penelope of trying to attract the notice of Essex. So one evening she and Penelope sat down to a cozy game of chess. The hand carved chess set cost $1,000. When it wasn't in use, they kept it in a fireproof vault at the studio.

Penelope on this occasion wore an inconspicuous little outfit of light blue satin, dripping with lace, a walloping diamond necklace with pearl drops, diamond earrings, and a head ornament plastered with gems. Elizabeth, also quietly garbed for an evening at home, wore a gold and green slashed gown weighted with perhaps a couple of quarts of diamonds, pearls, emeralds, rubies and sapphires. And a jewelled ostrich fan of red.

Well, in this chess game Elizabeth had the black knight (you play chess with queens, knights, castles and whatnot, remember?) and she said nastily: "So you would take the queen's knight, Mistress Penelope?"

"All knights are fair game, Your Grace," Penelope replied smartly.

"But," said Elizabeth, "the queen will protect her own—" and when Penelope was about to win, she swept all the chessmen to the floor!

Yet both women eventually lost the proud, head-strong Essex. Nobody who hears the Queen's voice in that final scene is likely to forget it. A few minutes before his execution, Essex refused his life at Elizabeth's hands, refused even her frantic offer to share the throne with him.

"No, Elizabeth: I'm over-ambitious—I'd be your death. And you, and England, must live." He turned toward the door; the massive portal of the royal suite in the Tower of London.

"Robert!" Elizabeth screamed, "take all! Take my crown! Take England!"

But Essex was gone. Presently from the courtyard rose the roll of drums, louder and louder. Then silence.

The stunned heartbreak on Elizabeth's face changed to mock indignation as Bette and Flynn left the set a moment later. Grinning, Flynn said something. Bette suddenly clutched her weighty skirts so that she could walk faster after him while Flynn hastened his stride to keep one step ahead of whatever reprisal she contemplated.

"I only said," Flynn broadcast with injured innocence, "Bette, if you could see how you don't look like yourself in that make-up, you wouldn't blame the guy for saying he'd rather die than marry you!' "

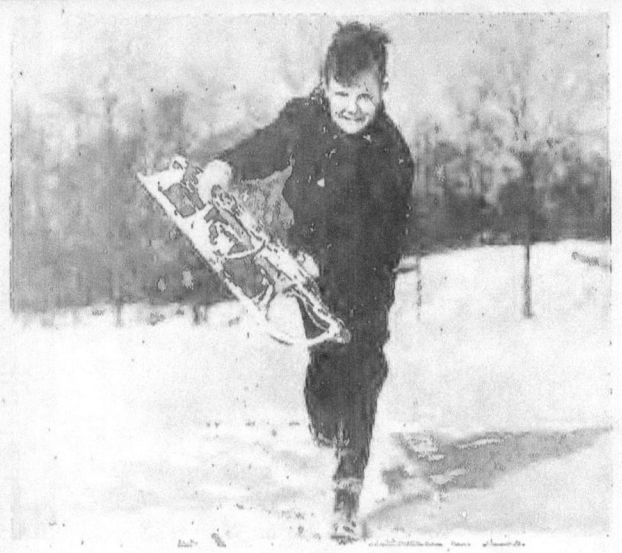

TO HELP WARD OFF SNIFFLES, many mothers start children on cod liver oil *early in the fall!* Many doctors say cod liver oil is unrivalled as a source of Vitamin A, so helpful in building resistance to common colds. And now THERE IS A BETTER WAY TO TAKE COD LIVER OIL . . . SCOTT'S EMULSION!

been more relaxed or felt better . . . and I've eaten lobsters and clams until they came out of my ears . . . and I've bought out all the antique shops for baby furniture for my sister's new heir . . . and I drove to Provincetown and saw a play that I'm crazy about . . . it's called *The Woman Brown* . . . and I wired Warner Bros. and they've bought it for me . . . and this place has changed since I was here ten years ago . . . and, oh, but it's fun to be back!"

Backstage and up a narrow flight of stairs to the third dressing room from the end, Bette led me.

"This was my very first dressing room in the theatre, when I played with Laura Hope Crews in *Mr. Pim Passes By*," she pointed with the pride of a mother exhibiting her first born. "And I shared it with Spring Byington. Bob Montgomery was on one side and Lloyd Nolan on the other.

We were a permanent company, with an occasional guest star.

"Being back here—seeing all this, do you wish that it was just beginning again for you?"

"Not by a long shot!" was Bette's explosive retort. "And don't let anyone ever kid you that they feel any differently. Going back into the past is just glamorous to say that they were much happier when they were starving in some cheap rooming house than they are now, when their income taxes make them cut down on caviar and champagne. It's good copy, but no more to be taken seriously than the sentimentalist who cries, 'Give me back the good old days!' What good old days? Before radio? Electric light? Telephone? Talking pictures? Television? Before there was a serum for pneumonia?

Before the Yankee Clipper and the Super-Chief? Before Helen Hayes?

"Coming back to Dennis was not a sentimental journey for me. I wasn't trying to recapture my early youth. I happen to adore the New England countryside—and I'm not being prejudiced because I'm a native New Englander. Most Americans ignore their own country. They'll travel days to see Amalfi Drive, the Cote d'Azur and the Scottish Lakes—when right in their own front yard they have Cape Cod, the Berkshires, New Hampshire, the Maine woods—scenery that is so breath-takingly beautiful, it almost hurts. I found the most divine spot at the foot of Sugar Hill, in Franconia, and I'm going to build a tiny rustic cabin on it, so that I can come to it on all my holidays.

"I know it's a terrific *cliche* to say that being in Hollywood for any length of time gets one into an awful rut, but unfortunately, it's true. It's like living on the Isle of Marken, in Holland, where everyone is related! We live in a private world of our own, with a large fence around it. International problems of the outside world pale into insignificance, compared to questions like "Will Cary Grant marry Phyllis Brooks?" or "Who has the most 'oomph'?" It is to get away from this insular way of living—to find a new mental stimulus, that most players feel the necessity of coming East once in a while. In the past, I've always made the mistake of coming directly to New York and tearing madly around, trying to see everything and everyone in a limited space of time. Consequently, when my 'vacation' was over, I found myself badly in need of another!

"This trip has been gloriously different. For the first time, I can honestly say that I'd be perfectly content not to work again for a whole year. As a matter of fact, I've already said it to Warner Bros."

"And what was the answer?"

"Well, I'm under suspension again—this time I'm fighting against making so many pictures each year. During the past year it was almost a game to find a theatre in which a Bette Davis picture was *not* playing! The result was that I reached the point where I was getting bored with thinking, breathing and eating pictures, and that's the danger signal for any actress! I'm trying to drive home this fact to the studio."

■ The curtain is lowered four times again to indicate the passing of a long lovely autumn, in which Bette ate New Hampshire farm cooking, swam in the ocean, caught mackerel with seventy-year-old Mr. Peckett, and went to the county fair.

By October, Bette was more enthusiastic than ever about the play, *The Woman Brown*, waiting for her in Hollywood. By November the rest cure was completed and she was back at the studio. By the time you read this, filming of her next picture, Rachel Fields' story, *All This and Heaven, Too*, will be under way. And by spring, Bette may have plans for her New England house complete, so that a "rest cure" will always be ready.

BETTE DAVIS and CHARLES BOYER

From the matchless pages of this brilliant best-seller comes a new chapter in film achievement! With all the incomparable artistry at their command these two great stars bring to life the deep-stirred emotions that burn from every excit ing word of the story!

You'll say when you see her that "Henriette" is a role heaven-sent just for Bette Davis! And you'll know, too, why Charles Boyer had to return all the way from France to play the impassioned Duc. For so many reasons this is the drama to be ranked in your memory with the topmost of all!

Included in the notable supporting cast are

JEFFREY LYNN • BARBARA O'NEIL

Virginia Weidler • Henry Daniell
Walter Hampden • George Coulouris

AN ANATOLE LITVAK PRODUCTION

Screen Play by Casey Robinson • Music by Max Steiner
A Warner Bros.-First National Picture

Warner Bros.
ARE HONORED TO OFFER
'ALL THIS AND HEAVEN TOO'
FROM THE WORLD-APPLAUDED NOVEL BY
Rachel Field

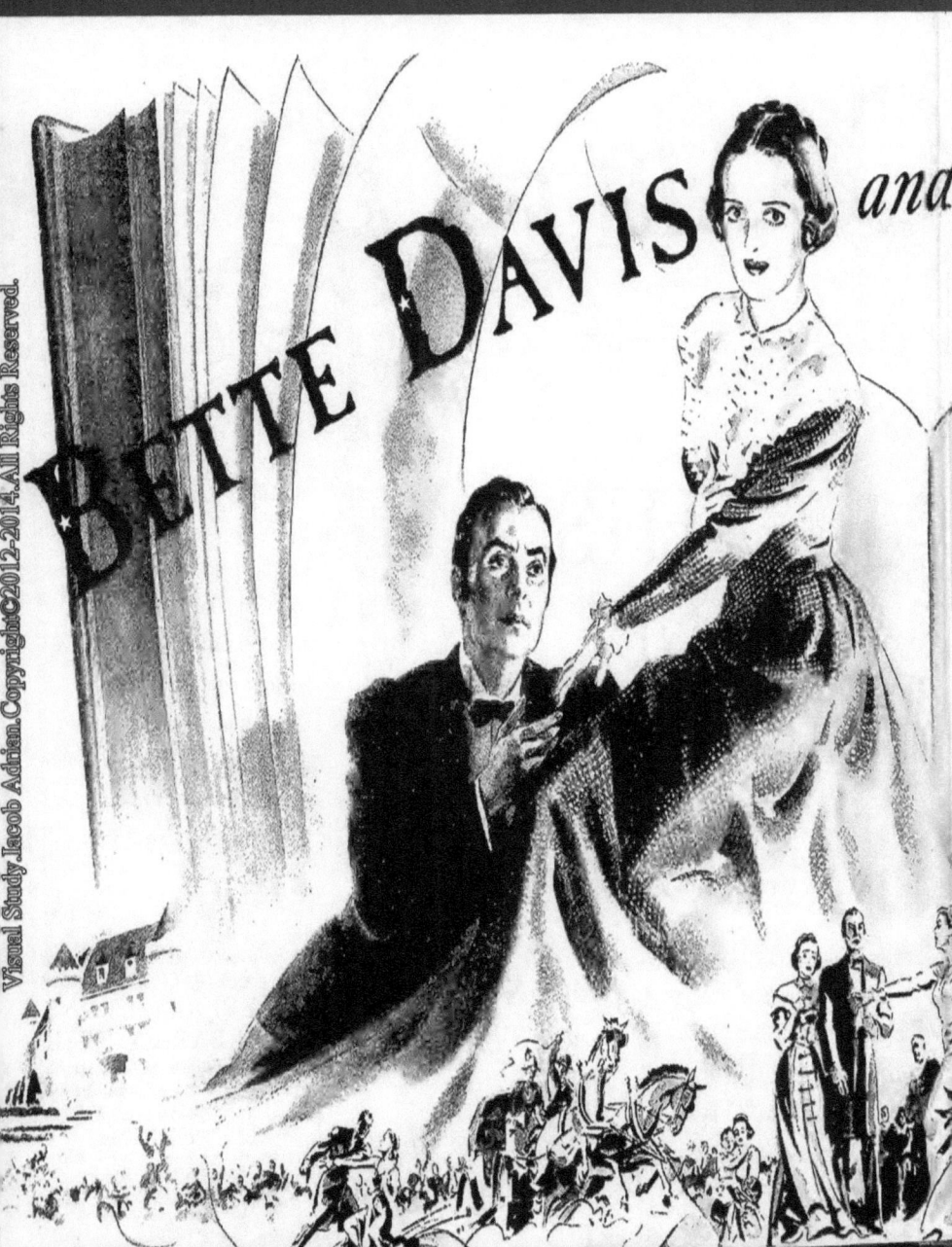

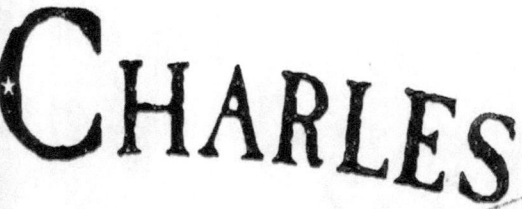

CHARLES BOYER

ALL THIS, AND HEAVEN TOO"

From the World-Applauded Novel By
Rachel Field

IN ALL ITS GLORY, with the full fire of its deep-stirring story, this beloved best-seller sweeps to the summit of screen achievement! And *never* have its stars come to you so immeasurably magnificent, or brought you a drama that touches so close to your heart. You will, of course, see it!

Especially distinguished in the supporting cast of this new WARNER BROS. Success, a

JEFFREY LYNN
BARBARA O'NEIL
Virginia Weidler • Henry Daniell
Walter Hampden • George Coulouris
*AN ANATOLE LITVAK
PRODUCTION*
Screen Play by Casey Robinson • Music by Max Steiner
A Warner Bros.-First National Picture

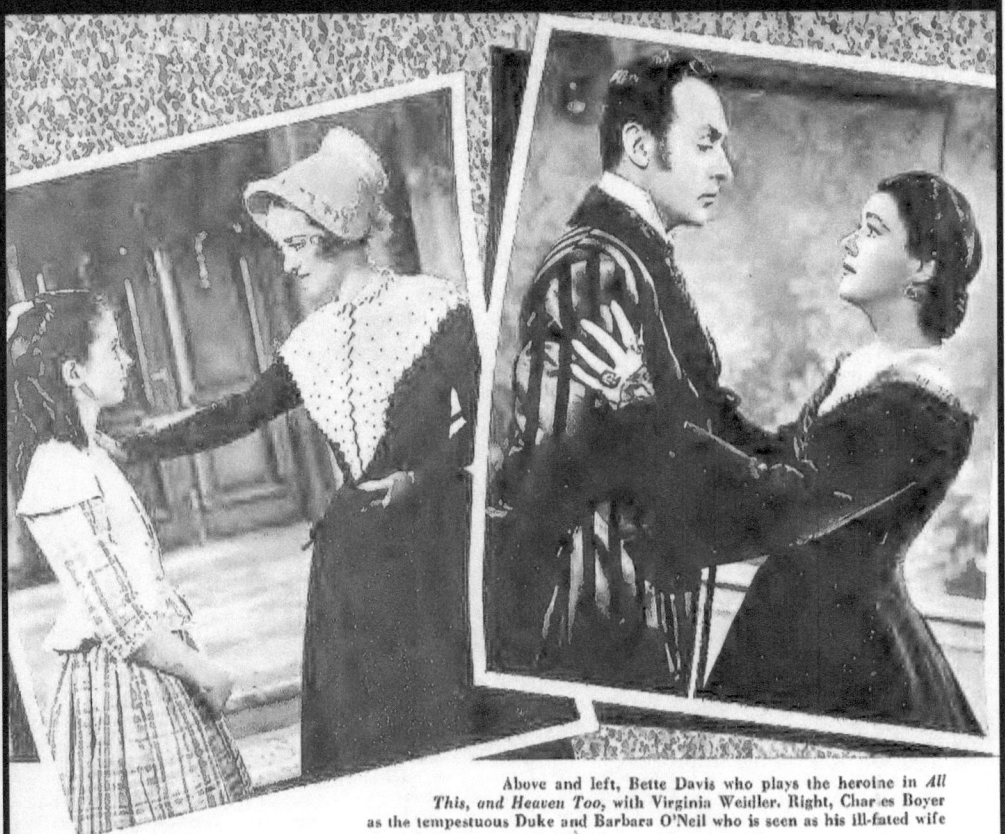

Above and left, Bette Davis who plays the heroine in *All This, and Heaven Too*, with Virginia Weidler. Right, Charles Boyer as the tempestuous Duke and Barbara O'Neil who is seen as his ill-fated wife

Tale of a Turbulent Triangle

By DUNCAN UNDERHILL

"Tonight," Mr. Charles Boyer exulted, a mischievous gleam lighting his normally slumberous eyes, "tonight is the night. Tonight I murder the duchess. Tonight I give her the beezness."

Mr. Boyer was referring to an incident in the eventful home life of Theobald, Duke of Praslin, who resided, toward the middle of the Nineteenth Century, at No. 55 Rue du Faubourg Saint-Honore, in the wonderful city of Paris. On the evening to which Mr. Boyer looked forward with so much relish Theobald, for reasons that seemed compelling at the time, slugged, cuffed and battered the life out of his noble Corsican wife, the mother of his ten children.

But the horrors did not cease there, as Mr. Boyer was only too happy to point out.

"Then I go to prison," he continued gaily, "and then I take strychnine and die and am buried in an unmarked grave in the prison yard. What a life! What a death!"

"What a picture!" an interested bystander might remark at this point.

Mr. Boyer's outburst of drollery was incidental to the making of a movie called *All This, and Heaven Too*, which deals with frustrated love, murder, the Atlantic Cable and related subjects.

These matters are all interwoven with the career of a certain Mlle. Henriette Desportes, who served the first half of her adulthood as a governess, latterly in the employ of the Duke and Duchess of Praslin, and the last half as the wife of a New York clergyman whose brother laid the Atlantic Cable.

The job of filming Henriette's turbulent life, as told in Rachel Field's best-selling novel, was a matter of compromise and condensation. No fictional character, but as vivid a human being as ever drew the breath of two republics, Mlle. Desportes lived twenty-six years of the Nineteenth Century in the United States. In the film this is cut down to a good sensible fifteen minutes of screen running time.

Some other notable corner-cuttings in the film are these:

In actuality, Theobald, the Duke of Praslin, was the progenitor of nine bouncing babies and one not so sprightly. The screenplay cuts this down to four, a fair enough numerical slash, since the ones retained in the story are Louise (Virginia Weidler), Raynald (Richard Nichols), Isabelle (June Lockhart), and Berthe (Ann Todd).

The illustrious American Field family, numbering eight sons and a daughter in the family album, is reduced by the Hollywood census-takers to four, of whom one appears on the screen and three as conversational props only.

Three of the greatest actors of all time, Rachel of the Comedie Francaise; Fanny Kemble and Edwin Booth, don't even appear in the movie, although each is given a jewel-box mounting in the book about Henriette Desportes on which the picture is based.

All this trim-

Tale of a Turbulent Triangle

ming and shearing leaves plenty of good solid footage for one of the most provocative triangles of all time. To make the elisions more bearable and the drama more intense, the Warner Brothers nominated Bette Davis to play Henriette. Mr. Boyer plays anchor man in the triangle, with Miss Davis as one of the emotional disturbances and Barbara O'Neil as the other.

As the Duchess of Praslin, this is Miss O'Neil's second performance in a twelve-month as Mr. Boyer's wife, the first having displayed her as a part-time lunatic in *When Tomorrow Comes*. In *All This, and Heaven Too*, she is a psychotic Corsican shrew, voluptuous, sultry and subject to moods veering from the calmly murderous to the violently suicidal.

A three-cornered tug-of-war among the top players might have been the reasonable expectation with such a set-up, with the director acting as referee. But as things worked out, each of the dominant trio proved to be such a deep-dyed professional actor that the prevailing tone was one of almost hysterical good nature, none of it forced or phony. Any of them who could have stood any more fun would have had to go to a hospital to recuperate.

Anatole Litvak, the directorial ringmaster of the three-ring circus, refused, like his players, to be daunted by exceptional circumstances. A congenital cigarette-man of championship calibre, Anatole is a difficult person to read behind his clouds of smoke. What may appear to be anger may be purely hunger, since he forgets his lunch unless somebody leads him to it and puts the tools in his hands.

Along about the second lap of production, after two unsuccessful takes of a pivotal scene, Anatole was heard to break out in his tone-deaf baritone:

"It's a hep-hep-heppy day!"

Under cover of the general laughter an assistant director remarked to a carpenter:

"A week behind schedule, the front office on his tail, and the old man can still sing. This picture is *in*, kid!"

◼ Miss Davis, carrying an inordinately heavy dramatic load on her slender shoulders, was seized simultaneously with attacks of mischief, laryngitis and the French language, with the result that for a few days she sounded like a slightly balmy basso immigrant.

Bette's mischief broke out when an admirer presented Mr. Boyer with a new make-up table. These things are ordinarily rough-and-ready, being constructed of an upright pipe mounted on a tripod with castors. The pipe supports a little shelf, an electrically lighted mirror, and just enough space to accommodate a brush, comb, powder puff, a pack of cigarettes and a deck of throat lozenges.

The Boyer gift, arriving while the star was at lunch, was a solidly constructed piece of furniture glittering with chromium like a modernistic hot dog stand. It had two drawers with combination locks, three hinged mirrors in ornate metal frames, and neon lights like a bar and grill.

Miss Davis, returning early from lunch, immediately appropriated this gem for her own use, moved all her set-side possessions onto it, switched Boyer's nameplate to her own broken-down table, and set her plate up on the razzle-dazzle contraption. Then she tipped off everybody in the company to tip off Boyer about the misdemeanor she had committed.

When the Frenchman returned to work he had heard the story from six sources. Miss Davis was primping ostentatiously when he passed her. He took no notice of her or the table and hasn't mentioned the larceny since. Miss Davis is wondering whether this is a subtle form of inverted French ribbing. If it is, she enjoys it as much as she does the luxury of her elegant new table.

◼ Playing her first French role, Miss Davis was suddenly conscience-stricken to realize that she knew practically nothing about the language. So she arranged to take lessons at odd moments from a top-ranking teacher.

One night at dinner hour, while there were still some scenes to be shot on the day's schedule, Bette and Director Litvak dropped in at the Blue Evening, a snack bar in the shadow of the studio. Bette was wearing slacks and goggles and Litvak was a stranger to the place.

They ordered a cocktail and a sandwich apiece and had half finished their snack when Bette suddenly remembered a fifteen-minute French lesson she had promised to wedge into the rest period.

Without pausing to explain why, she jumped up and left the restaurant. Litvak followed, thinking to drive her wherever she was bound. The manager of the Blue Evening went scurrying out the door after them, giving the impression to passersby that his place had just been knocked off by a gunman and his moll.

The net take of Litvak and his blond side-kick on that cafe job was $1.82 worth of food and drink. The sum was contributed to the house cash register by philanthropic Warnerites eager to preserve the good name of the studio. Litvak and Bette do not realize yet that they are a couple of delinquents.

◼ A freak of the shooting schedule of *All This, and Heaven Too*, set up a big emotional scene between Bette and Barbara O'Neil for nine o'clock in the morning. Barbara was up on her lines and began pitching them with true Corsican venom at 9:02, Pacific Time. Bette's sense of humor overtook her again at this point and she burst into laughter.

"This is too stark," she announced to the assembled company. "Let's have a pot of coffee, a cigarette, and a few laughs all around. It will probably prevent homicide later in the day. If we start off at this pitch we'll be at each other's throats in earnest by nightfall."

Rachel Field, the author, visited the set twice and both times made a special point of placing a laurel wreath on the brow of Casey Robinson, the adapter of her best-selling book. It will be Miss Field's first work to reach the screen, although a novel of hers, *Time Out of Mind*, is resting comfortably in the literary vault at Universal.

Miss Field was frankly astounded by the courtesy and friendliness with which she was greeted by the players, the producer and the director.

"I had no idea," she confessed, "that picture people would make me feel so utterly at home. I had understood that if I ventured a foot within the studio gates my name would be Rachel Anathema."

With entire good grace Miss Field accepted the nomination of two players far different physically from their counterparts in her book and in real life. The Duke of Praslin, as the House of Peers and the French police knew him, was tall and his hair was the color of cornsilk. Henry Field, as the family annals have it, was a runt.

Yet it isn't every day that you can reach out and get Charles Boyer to play a duke for you, and if he happens to look more like Napoleon Bonaparte than a Norse god, what harm does that do to anybody?

Jeffrey Lynn is a good foot taller than Henry Field, Henriette's eventual bridegroom, but why be picayune about details when Jeffrey makes such an earnest and convincing young ecclesiastic?

Among the remainder of the cast there is plenty of accurate type-casting: Montagu Love as a dour Corsican marshal, the father of the duchess; Fritz Leiber as a conspiratorial abbe, and Edward Fielding as a physician.

Barbara O'Neil conforms closest of all the principals to the historic specifications. As a great but erratic lady of the court of Louis Philippe, she comports herself in truly ducal style. As in two other recent pictures, one with Boyer and one with Edward G. Robinson, she is compelled, in *All This, and Heaven Too*, to play many of her scenes in stocking feet.

In the past Miss O'Neil's height has been a drawback to her. In the future, it seems likely, pictures will be especially designed for her, so that no incongruity may arise.

Bette Davis, of course, can be anybody she wants to be, from Queen Elizabeth to Queen Mab, with no dissenting votes from any quarter. Amid a warehouseful of Empire furniture and period costumes, you can be assured that Miss Davis is running up an early point score toward her periodical Academy Award.

The law of averages catches up with everybody some time. Miss Davis may do a bad picture some time. But *All This, and Heaven Too*, advances her one more mile in her orderly progression toward the actors' Olympus.

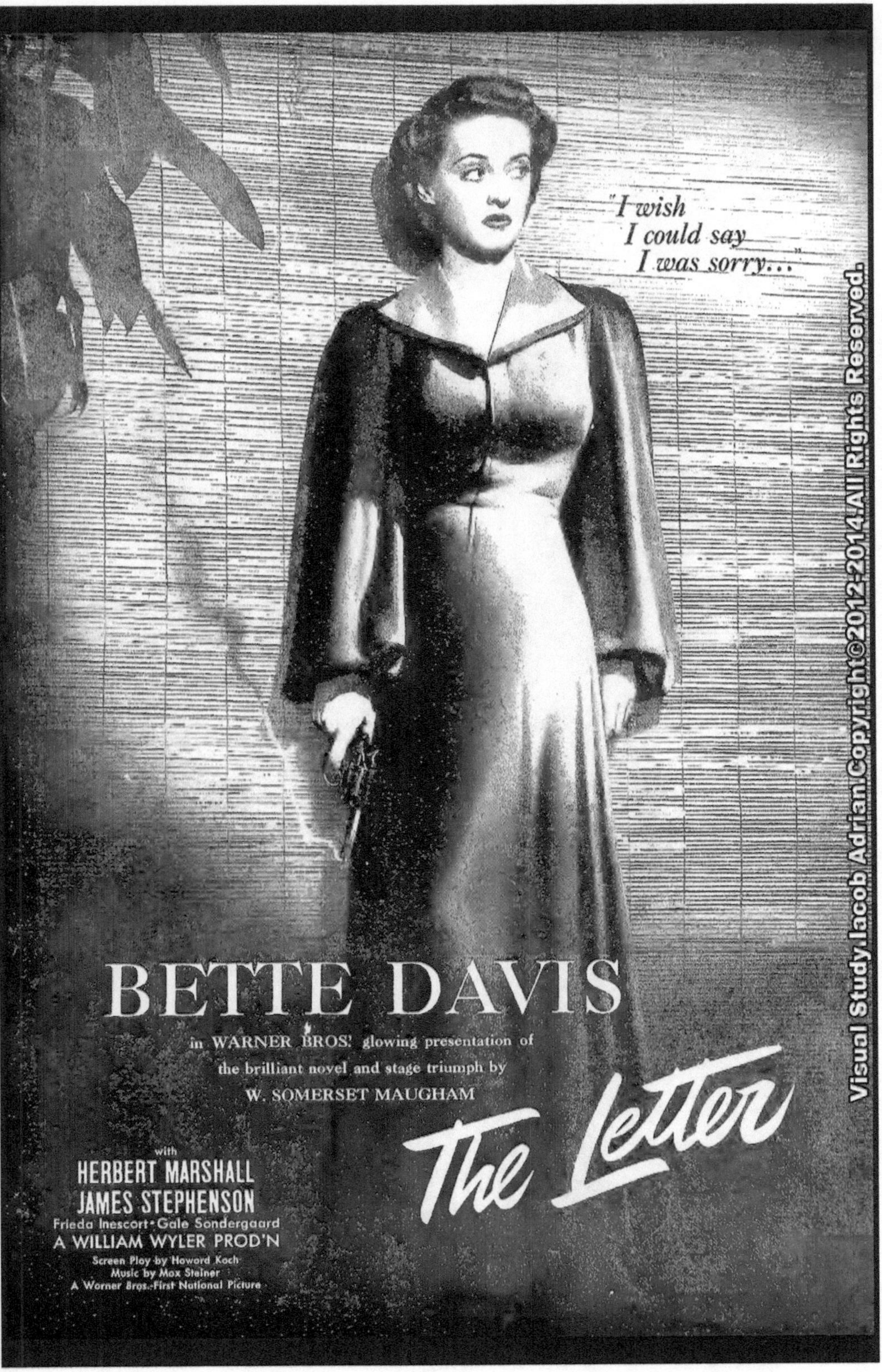

"I wish I could say I was sorry…"

BETTE DAVIS

in WARNER BROS! glowing presentation of
the brilliant novel and stage triumph by

W. SOMERSET MAUGHAM

The Letter

with
HERBERT MARSHALL
JAMES STEPHENSON
Frieda Inescort • Gale Sondergaard
A WILLIAM WYLER PROD'N
Screen Play by Howard Koch
Music by Max Steiner
A Warner Bros.-First National Picture

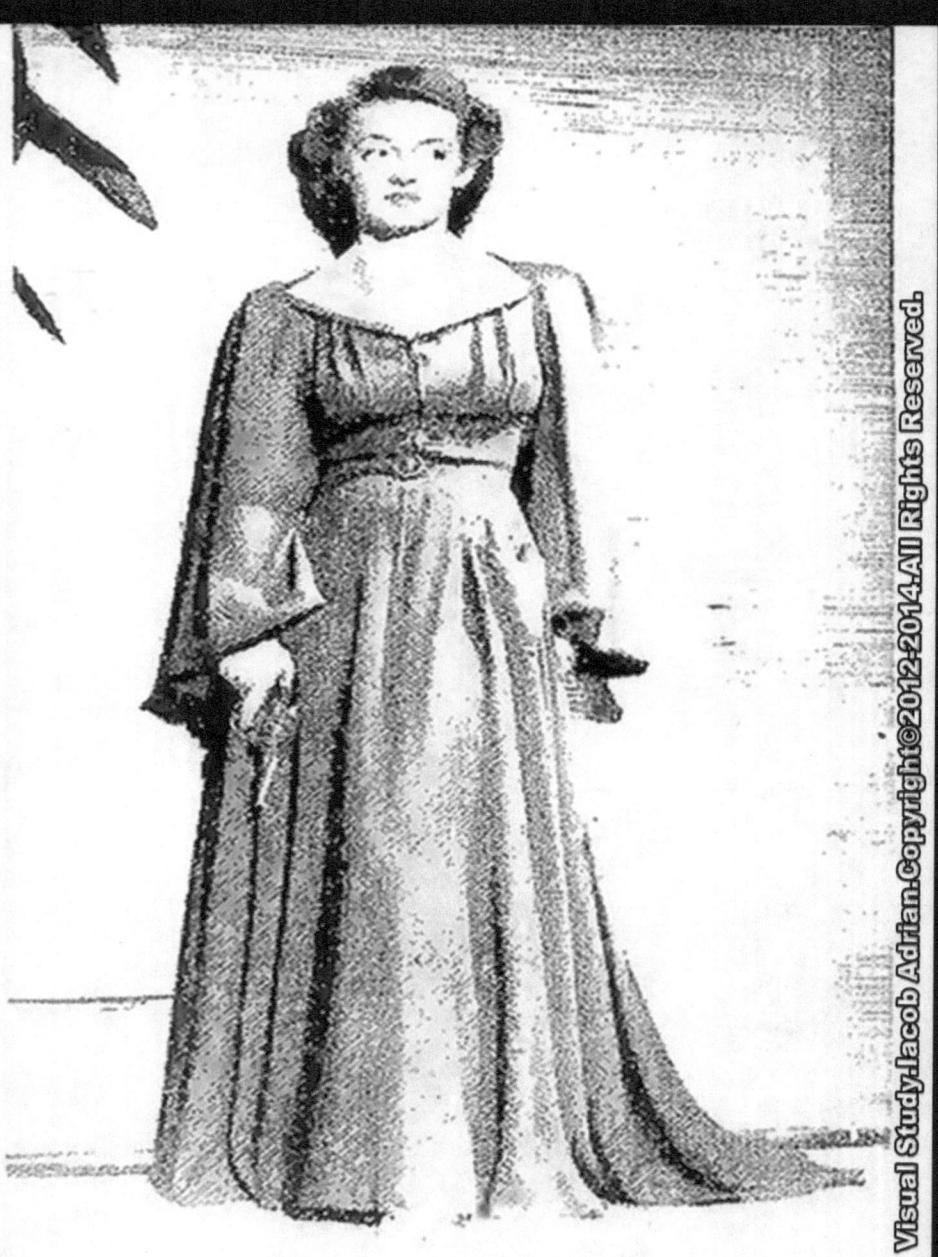

There is gunplay of all kinds all over the Warner Brothers' lot. Here is Bette Davis thinking over some direct action for her role in *The Letter*

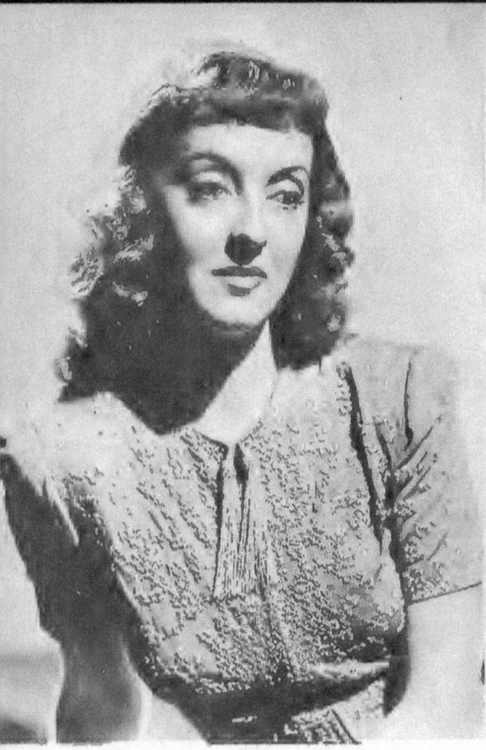

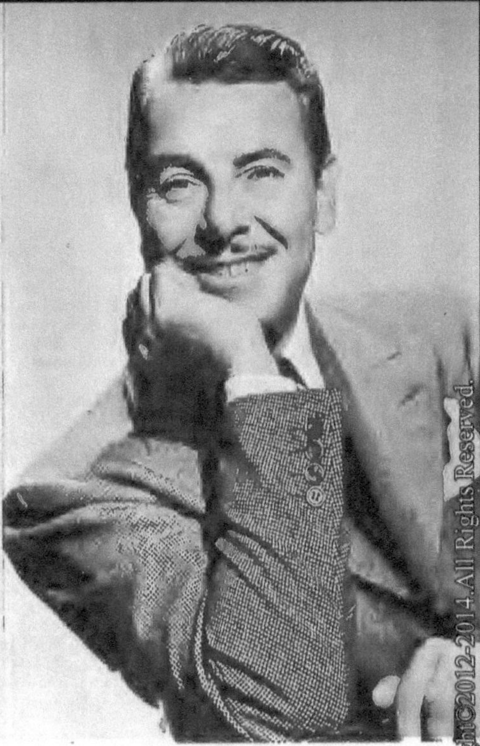

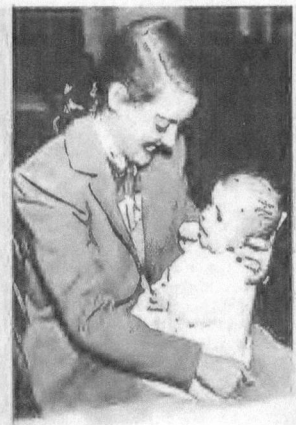
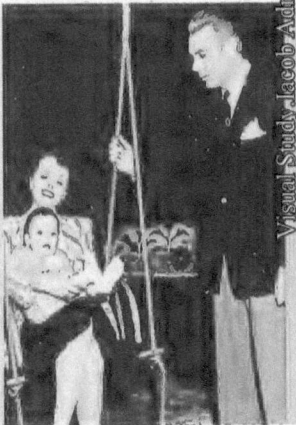

Bette Davis and George Brent co-star in *The Great Lie*. Contrary to former Davis patterns, Bette's new film does not find her killing anyone, acting nasty or wearing wigs and period costumes. This is Bette's first opportunity in a long time to appear glamorous on the screen—and she really goes to town! She makes innumerable costume changes and even has a new coiffure

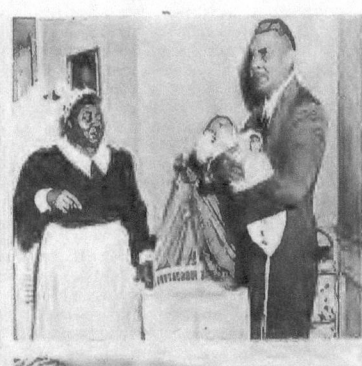

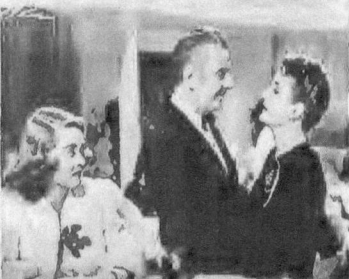

Above: Young Billy Ferris, around whom plot revolves, claims Bette's undivided attention. Top center: George Brent, Hattie McDaniels and Billy in a scene from the new picture. Powder dusted in his hair has aged Brent for this particular scene

Above: Mary Astor, the film's "other woman" is the cause for Brent's unhappiness. Left: The three principals of the triangle, Bette, George and Mary. During the production of her new film, Bette surprised everyone by becoming Mrs. Arthur Farnsworth

Bette Davis Turns Softie

By JACK HOLLAND

■ Blissful as a new-born babe I dashed across the set of *The Great Lie.* I had no mercenary ideas in mind. I just wanted to see what was going on and to talk to Bette Davis. Suddenly I heard someone from a far corner of the set call out, "Hi!" I looked up and practically fell through the floor. There was Bette lying in bed. I personified a nervous smile and started to leave. Then, realizing that business knows no obstacles, I walked directly over to her. Tibbie, her Scottie, who was posing menacingly on the bed, didn't understand business, for he let go with a growl. ' Bette finally quieted him. Just then there was a call for Bette on the set. She got out of bed, excused herself, and on her way to take the call said to me, "Isn't this the cutest outfit I've got on?" I had turned my back when she got out of bed, but when a lady asks you to look at her outfit—well. . . . There she was dressed in a complete riding habit, sans the boots, of course. What a "get-up" to sleep in!

And what a first impression of one of Warners' biggest 1941 productions.

A few moments later, Bette was back. "You know, when I first started to make *The Great Lie,* I wasn't very excited about it. I had just come back from my vacation at my new ranch in New Hampshire and the studio had asked me to make some added scenes for *The Letter.* Then I was informed I would have to cut my hair before I began work on this picture. I was so upset that I almost decided to turn down the role. I was still wondering what to do when I got some of my fan mail. A lot of it ran in this vein: 'Why can't you be nice for a change?' 'Why must you always be a heel?' Then I remembered what some people in New Hampshire said when they saw me recently: 'Why, gee whiz! You're *young!*' Everyone apparently had the idea that I was an old hag, judging from the many character parts I've played.

"That decided me, and now I'm glad I'm making *The Great Lie.* I guess I do need happier roles for a change. You know, I don't kill a soul in this picture, and I'm not even selfish or mean."

Bette was called away for a scene with George Brent. I watched it for a while and began to wonder just how sweet Bette was supposed to be. Boy! was she telling George off! What a fight! But suddenly, Bette began to laugh. Eddie Goulding, the director, said, "Cut!" The scene started again. After a while, Bette got the giggles once more.

"I'm sorry, Eddie, but it's George's fault," Bette said, coming over to Goulding. "Drat him anyway. He gets a certain look in his eyes, and I can't go on."

To which George hurriedly replied, "She giggles. I don't do a thing. She just quits fighting and giggles."

"All right, you happy warriors," Eddie said, "let's try it again."

Such is the way Bette and George work. They're probably the most genially compatible stars in Hollywood.

The story of *The Great Lie,* which is based on Polan Banks' novel, *Far Horizon* is not quite as compatible, however. It's a triangle affair, full of pathos, babies, mother love, tears, drama, and all the trimmings.

The drama begins when *Peter Van Allen* (George Brent), a playboy aviator, wakes up after a ten-day binge to discover he's married to *Sandra Kovac* (Mary Astor), a concert pianist. But *Peter* loves *Maggie* (Bette Davis). When everything looks hopeless, *Peter* is momentarily saved when he learns that his marriage to *Sandra* is illegal since she hadn't as yet received her final divorce decree from her previous marriage. *Peter* rushes to *Maggie's* Maryland plantation. She refuses to forgive him for what he's done, so he hops in his plane, goes back to *Sandra,* and in his plight asks her to marry him, legally. She says she'd like to, but that her forthcoming concert won't permit her to take another jump in the sea of matrimony for a while. So *Peter* rushes back to *Maggie* again. She forgives him. And they are married.

Their happiness is short-lived, for *Peter* is called away by the government to make a South American survey flight. *Maggie* goes with him to Washington to see him off. There she meets *Sandra. Sandra* informs her that she is expecting a baby— *Peter's* baby. *Maggie,* confused, afraid *Sandra* is using the baby angle only to get *Peter* back, doesn't know what to do. Then comes word that *Peter's* plane has gone down in the jungle and that little hope is held for any of the survivors.

Maggie then insists that *Sandra* accompany her to a ranch in Arizona where they will both await the baby's arrival. There, *Maggie* acts as guardian to *Sandra's* health, bullies her, pampers her. In due time, the baby arrives. It's a boy—named *Peter. Maggie* gets *Sandra* to give her the baby after an argument and after *Sandra* considers a proposed concert tour more important than being a mother. Suddenly, *Peter Van Allen* returns, alive and well. He thinks the baby is his and *Maggie's.* She says nothing, afraid to tell him the truth. Upon the scene a few days later comes *Sandra,* ready to bare the whole business, to get *Peter* back.

The solution to the dilemma has some surprise moments, so the final outcome will not be bared here.

■ The various locales used in the picture certainly provided a problem for the technical directors. Bette's Maryland plantation was scattered over a half a dozen sound stages at Warners and some 50 acres of Southern California landscape. The kitchen wing and side yard occupied all of stage 22. Bette's bedroom was on another stage, the living room on a third, and the remaining interiors on three more.

The kitchen was another interesting item. It was completely decked out with everything from copper kettles, pans, and the like to jars of preserves, jams, and canned fruit.

"Seeing those jars of fruit," Bette said, "brings back poignant memories. When I was back home in New Hampshire recently, I put up a lot of jelly. I just heard a few days ago that every jar of jelly had broken and spilled all over the place. I still don't know whether it was because of the cold snap or just my own bad technique."

Bette led me to the graceful stairway used in the picture as we continued our tour of the sets. "You know," she said, "this is the same stairway that was used in *Jezebel* and *The Old Maid.* The set decorators always try to fool me by disguising it, but I'm never fooled. I'm quite alert on this decorating business, for I've been doing a lot of sketches for my own home in Glendale and for my farm in New Hampshire.

"This is my ghost room," Bette continued as we came to a secluded set on the sound stage. "I made my entrance in *Jezebel* in this room, died here in *Dark Victory,* and killed a man here in *The Letter.* This time I make love to George Brent in it."

I left Bette at her dressing room and went wandering around alone. Suddenly I overheard George Brent and Jerome Cowan talking behind the cameras.

"How's the bridegroom?" Cowan asked.

"Don't you start that," Brent roared. "Ann Sheridan and I are not married. I can't imagine where that rumor began."

Cowan looked puzzled. "As far as I'm concerned," he said, "it started in the script. That's my first line in our scene. We were rehearsing, remember?"

An overly-hued George was called, propitiously, to do a scene with Hattie McDaniels, the unforgettable *Mammy* of *G.W.T.W.* He was in a perfect spot to do some nifty blow-ups. But he didn't.

Hattie McDaniels recently received a certificate of merit from the National Memorial to Advancement of the Colored Race, naming her as leading colored actress of the stage and screen. The certificate was

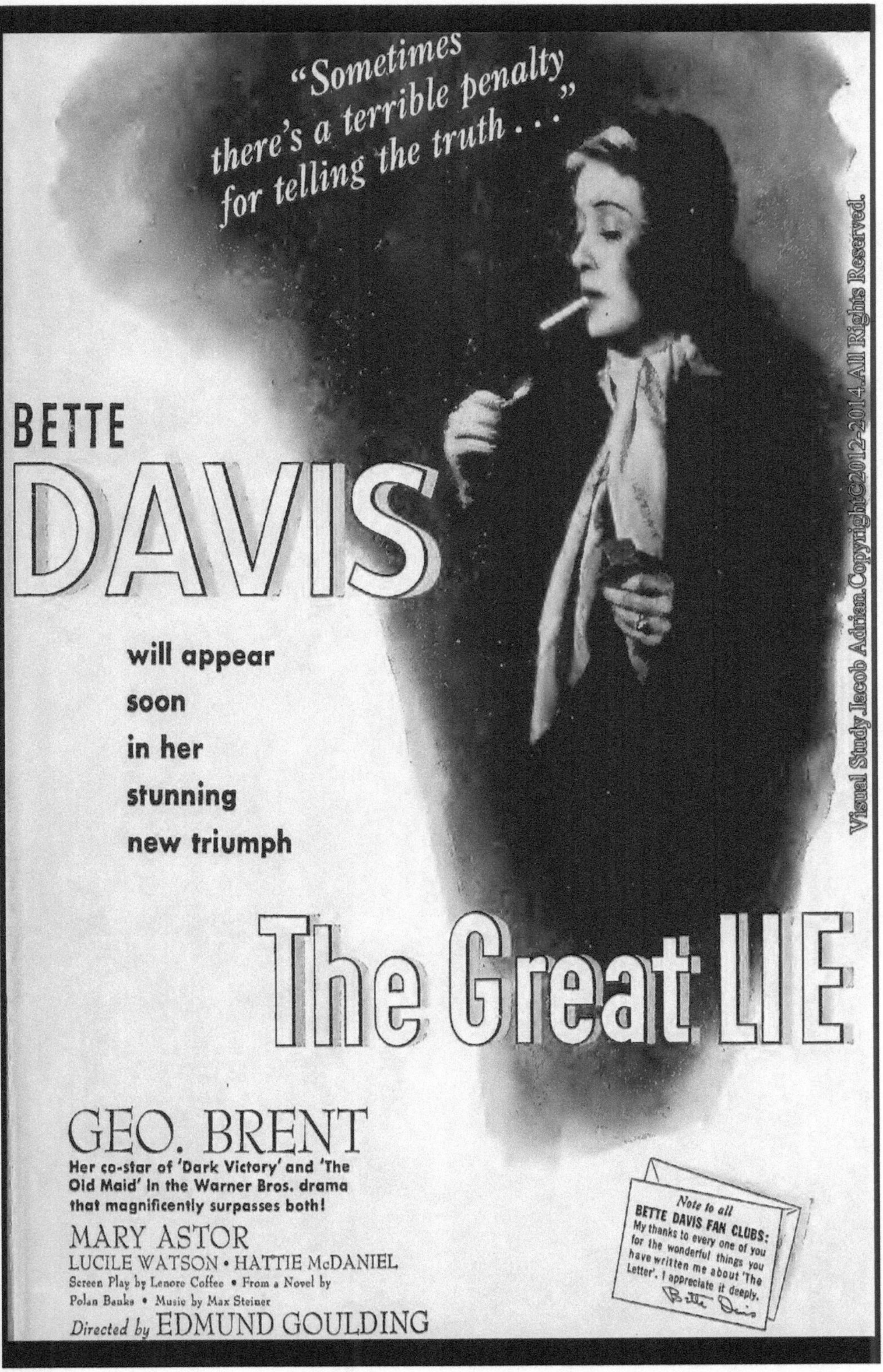
"Sometimes
there's a terrible penalty
for telling the truth . . ."
BETTE
DAVIS
will appear
soon
in her
stunning
new triumph
The Great LIE
GEO. BRENT
Her co-star of 'Dark Victory' and 'The Old Maid' in the Warner Bros. drama that magnificently surpasses both!
MARY ASTOR
LUCILE WATSON • HATTIE McDANIEL
Screen Play by Lenore Coffee • From a Novel by Polan Banks • Music by Max Steiner
Directed by EDMUND GOULDING
Note to all
BETTE DAVIS FAN CLUBS:
My thanks to every one of you for the wonderful things you have written me about 'The Letter'. I appreciate it deeply.
Bette Davis

JAMES CAGNEY

← BETTE DAVIS

having the
time of their
lives in the
best picture of
their lives,

"THE BRIDE
CAME C.O.D."

(Warner Bros. produced it)

Isn't it wonderful!—
both in the same picture!!

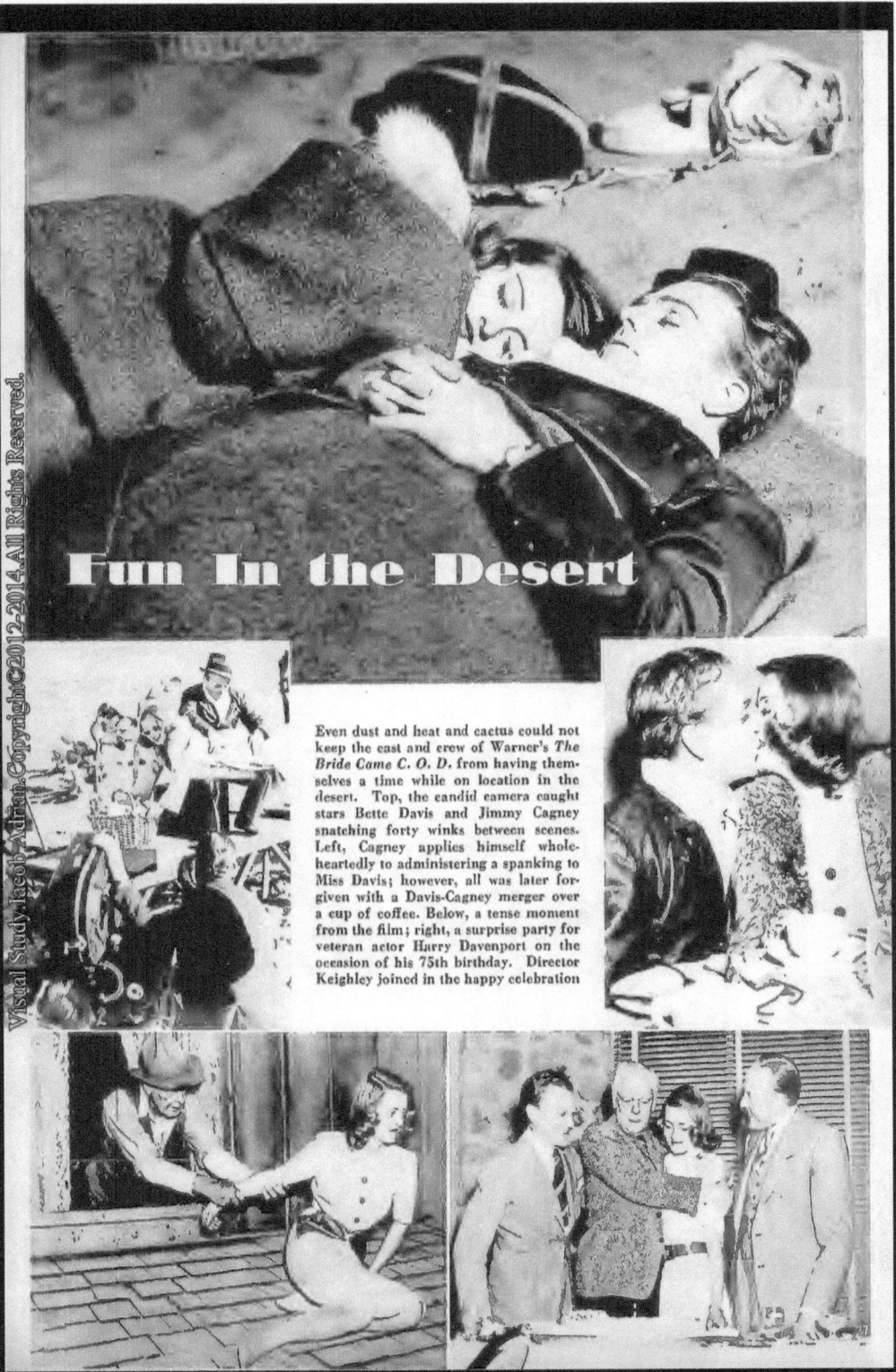

Fun In the Desert

Even dust and heat and cactus could not keep the cast and crew of Warner's *The Bride Came C. O. D.* from having themselves a time while on location in the desert. Top, the candid camera caught stars Bette Davis and Jimmy Cagney snatching forty winks between scenes. Left, Cagney applies himself whole-heartedly to administering a spanking to Miss Davis; however, all was later forgiven with a Davis-Cagney merger over a cup of coffee. Below, a tense moment from the film; right, a surprise party for veteran actor Harry Davenport on the occasion of his 75th birthday. Director Keighley joined in the happy celebration

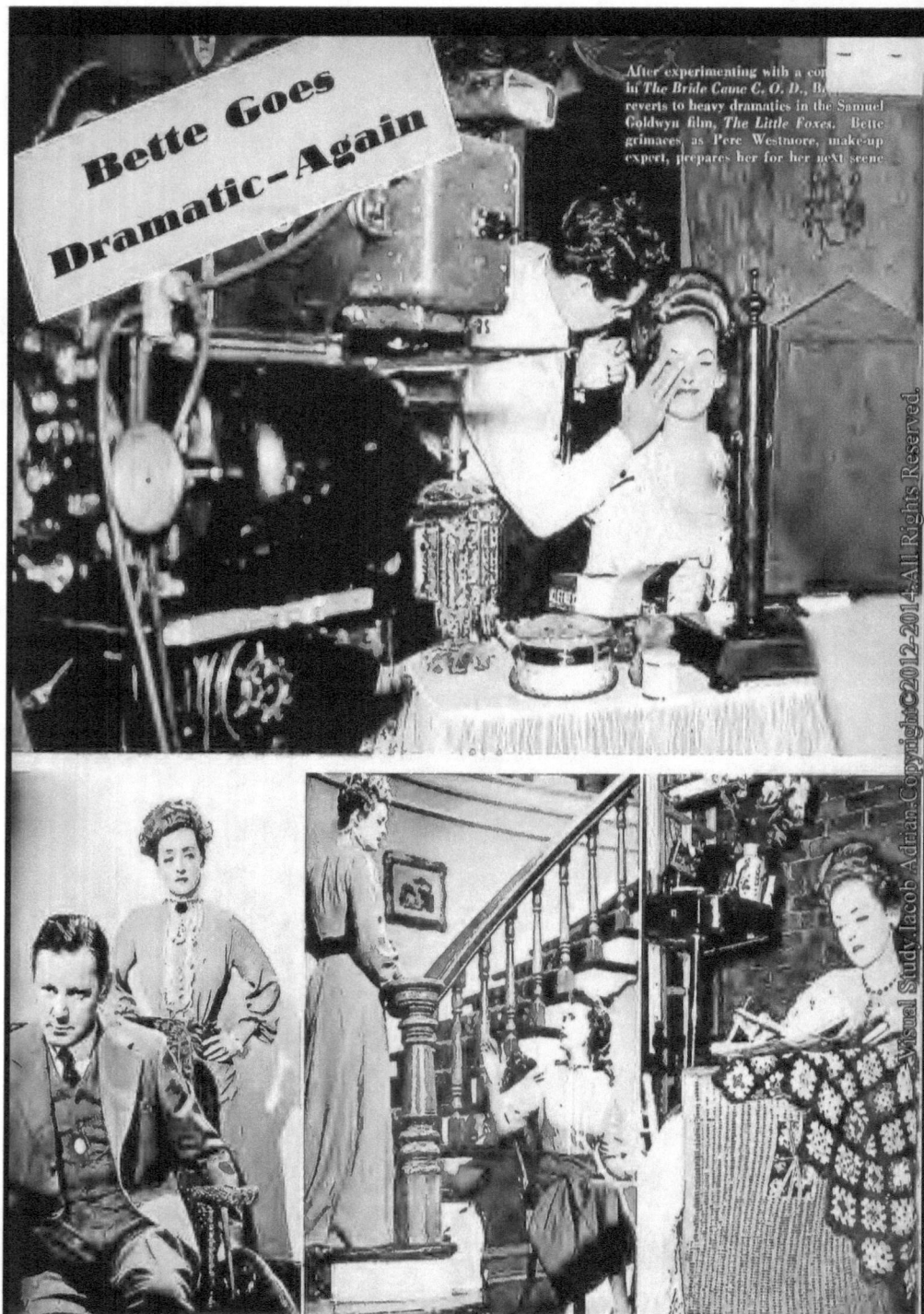

Bette Goes Dramatic—Again

After experimenting with a com... in *The Bride Came C. O. D.*, B... reverts to heavy dramatics in the Samuel Goldwyn film, *The Little Foxes*. Bette grimaces, as Perc Westmore, make-up expert, prepares her for her next scene

Herbert Marshall, Bette's invalid husband, tries desperately to prevent her from ruining their daughter's life

Alexandra (Theresa Wright) defies her unscrupulous mother in this dramatic scene, directed by William Wyler

With the tired lines magically erased from her face, Miss Davis relaxes between scenes with a copy of a current best-seller

By HELEN HOVER

Bette Davis —

When Bette Davis discovered Richard Travis, HOLLYWOOD immediately assigned Helen Hover to get the story which appears on this page. However, Bette pulled a fast one on us, and set to work discovering John Sutton, whose story, written by John Franchey, appears on the opposite page. There seems to be no stopping the Davis lady, for a last minute flash brings word that Bette's latest "find" is Ernest Anderson, a young Negro singer, who was given a role in Bette's forthcoming picture, "In This Our Life."   The Editor

Now to look at strapping six-foot-two Richard Travis, you'd say he was the last person in the world who needed someone to push him. He's a cross between Joel McCrea, Gary Cooper and Billy Conn—which makes him a fellow who can take care of himself.

But the truth must be told: the direct force which changed Richard overnight from a nobody to a coming star, from a mouse to a man, is a nervous little 103-pound blonde named Bette Davis.

To show you how trifling are the circumstances on which a person's Fate hinges: If Bette Davis hadn't wanted her steak well-done instead of medium rare one evening, Travis would still be an obscure young hopeful instead of a promising leading man who makes his debut in The Man Who Came to Dinner.

Bette and her husband, Arthur Farnsworth, were having dinner prior to attending the opening of The Bride Came C.O.D. Bette returned her steak for an extra once-over. That caused a delay of ten minutes and when Bette arrived at the theater she had missed the beginning of the picture. That was to change Richard Travis' life!

Ordinarily, Bette leaves right after the main feature, but this time she whispered to Arthur, "Let's sit through the entire show. I want to see the beginning." So they sat through the newsreel. Then a movie short on national defense followed. Bette slumped into her seat. Suddenly, she sat up briskly, her eyes fixed on a good-looking, blond husky on the screen. The next morning Bette walked into the executive office of Warner Brothers and insisted that the young man be given a test for the romantic lead in The Man Who Came to Dinner!

Bette has always believed that new talent should be developed, in spite of the fact that such a philosophy might endanger her own security. Her judgment is held high at the studio, so the boy was given a chance.

And that is how, one recent morning, Richard Travis happened to be called to the hall phone of the boarding house where he shared a $35 a month apartment with two other fellows, and heard the order to report to Warner Brothers to test for The Man Who Came to Dinner. "Huh?" grunted Richard groggily. But the caller had hung up.

Now we must interrupt the little drama here and introduce our bewildered hero. At this point, Richard Travis was one of thousands of handsome young men trying to crash into pictures and getting nowhere. He had come from Paragould, Arkansas, a shy, ambitious small town boy, with no connections and no theatrical background. That morning, just before he received the telephone call, he wrote his folks that he was coming home.

He wasn't the type who looked like an actor, anyway. A brief appearance in a high school play had made him stage-struck, and he followed that up by working in the town's movie house where he functioned as head usher and setter of the marquee lights. Then he made a trip to Hollywood to test his chances. He met Josephine Dillon, famous Hollywood coach who trained and was once married to Clark Gable. She looked him over like a racehorse on the auction block. "Hmmm—clean and wholesome type. You're the kind every girl likes for a boy friend and every fellow likes for a pal," she told him, while Dick reddened. "I'll teach you to act, but you must promise me never to change. Remain nice and natural because if I find you going hammy or Hollywood on me, so help me, I'll send you back to Arkansas."

She advised him to join a little theater group, and through that he was given a small part in a defense short called, Here Comes the Cavalry. The part wasn't big, the pay wasn't much and the whole thing didn't dent the sensibilities of any producers. The job over, Dick was out of work, moping in the apartment one morning, wondering where he'd be going from here—when he was called to the phone! He walked slowly back to the apartment and told his two roommates that Warner Brothers wanted to test him for Bette Davis' next picture.

"Miss Davis herself recommended me," he said.

"Someone must be ribbing you," they hooted.

Dick thought that too on his way to the studio. It must be a joke. But strangely enough, the receptionist recognized his name, had him ushered to a sound stage where everyone was waiting for him to make his test.

Remembering her own bitter struggle to gain a foothold in Hollywood, Bette Davis goes out of her way to give promising beginners a helping hand. She is shown with one of her discoveries, Richard Travis, who has a fine role in Bette's film, The Man Who Came to Dinner

Talent Scout

"I was in a daze—in so much of a daze that I didn't have sense enough to be nervous," explains Richard, still a little baffled by his luck. "When I was told later that the test had won me a big role in The Man Who Came to Dinner, I just turned around like a sleepwalker, wired the folks that something had hit me on the head and I hadn't awakened yet."

He was promptly initiated into the hectic routine of being transformed into a prominent leading man. He was photographed and interviewed by the press. A stand-in and a secretary were hired for him.

"I can understand the stand-in," he said. "But why the secretary?"

"Oh, to handle your fan clubs," was the nonchalant answer. He reeled.

His real name, Bill Justice, was changed to Richard Travis for no apparent reason, since Bill Justice suits his virile handsomeness much better. He can't get used to the new name, so Bette Davis still calls him "Bill" to make him feel at home.

"All this fuss over me," says Bill blinking. "Imagine Bette Davis calling me 'Bill.' Why I used to set her name up on the marquee of the Paragould movie house last year. The folks in Arkansas wouldn't believe me. I had to send them a picture of me and Miss Davis together!"

By
JOHN FRANCHEY

Heaven knows what would have happened to John Sutton if it hadn't been for Bette Davis. And as for Susan (the very thought of it is enough to make you shudder!), she probably would have ended up a tramp.

This is how Bette managed to rescue the Sutton gentleman from himself and to save him for the movies.

The time was mid-afternoon; the scene, Stage 11 on the Warner lot; the picture in production, a costume piece called Elizabeth and Essex. Miss Davis, of course, was playing Elizabeth. According to the script Miss Davis was to be encountered by a very minor character designated as the "Captain of the Guard." He was to dash in, salute, pay his respects, say a few lines, click his heels, and then beat it.

Well, there she was all set for the captain of the guard to show up and make his microscopic speech so she could get on to a more dramatic scene with Errol Flynn when all of a sudden in dashed a knightly figure, pranced up to her, flashed his eyes in her direction, saluted like a real soldier, spoke his lines with a manly abandon, and disappeared.

"Who was that?" Miss Davis, somewhat out of breath, asked the assistant director.

"John Sutton. He does occasional bits."

"Only bits?"

"That's right. He doesn't seem to give a darn."

Later that afternoon Bette Davis and John Sutton met for a chat. Bette wanted to find out more about this man Sutton. She did.

She asked him what he did between bits and was astounded to discover that he spent his time "looking for a job." What kind of a job? Any old job. Just so long as he and Susan had a roof over their heads. Didn't he have an ambition? None especially; he didn't have any qualifica-

Smiling John Sutton owes his new star classification and attractive contract to Bette Davis, who insisted he buckle down to work. John appeared in 20th Century-Fox's A Yank in the R.A.F., and more recently as the male lead in Moon Over Her Shoulder

tions. What about that military manner of his? Oh, that. He had picked it up at Sandhurst Military Academy in England. What about acting as a career? He wasn't cut out to be an actor. He did bit parts simply because he could find no other jobs.

This is where Bette Davis saved him from himself. She told him that as an actor he had fine possibilities. She was sure of that merely from what she had seen him do that afternoon. She thought he ought to give acting a real try. Furthermore, she would do all she could to help.

That pep talk from Bette Davis did the trick. He went home to Susan a new man,

determined to give Miss Davis' theory a real tryout, just as soon as his ten-day stint in Elizabeth and Essex was over.

Bette went to bat for him the very next day with the Warner front office. The Warner chiefs listened very patiently and said they'd keep him in mind.

She talked to the big boys over at T.C.-F. They said they'd test him the first chance they got. Meanwhile, she passed the word around to every studio in town.

That talking campaign of hers bore quick fruit. Hardly had he kissed the Warner paymaster good-bye when he got a call from Universal. They wanted to test him for a part in Towers of London.

He took the test, got the part, landed a contract, and settled down to the business of becoming an actor.

That role in Towers of London was a killer. He played the part of a tinsel hero who was, in his own words, "a blooming bore who saved the queen's jewels and won the girl, only God knows why, in the end."

He hung around doing small roles over at Universal until he began to wonder if maybe Bette Davis had thrown him a curve in suggesting that he get serious with pictures. In time, he was shoved into a picture called, I Can't Give You Anything But Love, Baby, in which he played a stooge to Broderick Crawford. Sutton quit Universal when his year was up and there he and Susan were once more, at sixes and sevens.

For two months he waited for a call from someone who might need a slightly disillusioned captain of the guard, and not one yip out of Susan, the ever-understanding. At the end of the ninth week he noticed she was getting slimmer.

At which point, just like in the movies, a call came in the nick of time from the boys over at Twentieth Century-Fox, the very boys whom Miss Davis had worked on. It seems that an outdoor saga called Hudson's Bay was going into production and needed someone along the lines described by Miss Davis. Mr. Sutton dropped by the next morning, got the test, the part, Gene Tierney for a heroine, and a wave of favorable mention from the critics for the nice job he did.

The John Sutton whose performance in A Yank in the R.A.F. has brought him a memo, with gold star attached, from Darryl Zanuck, has a background which explains his diffidence to the movies up until the time Bette Davis gave him that pep talk. The man certainly has lived, as they say.

He was born in Rawalpindi, India, the scion of a com-

"Rest Cure" For Bette

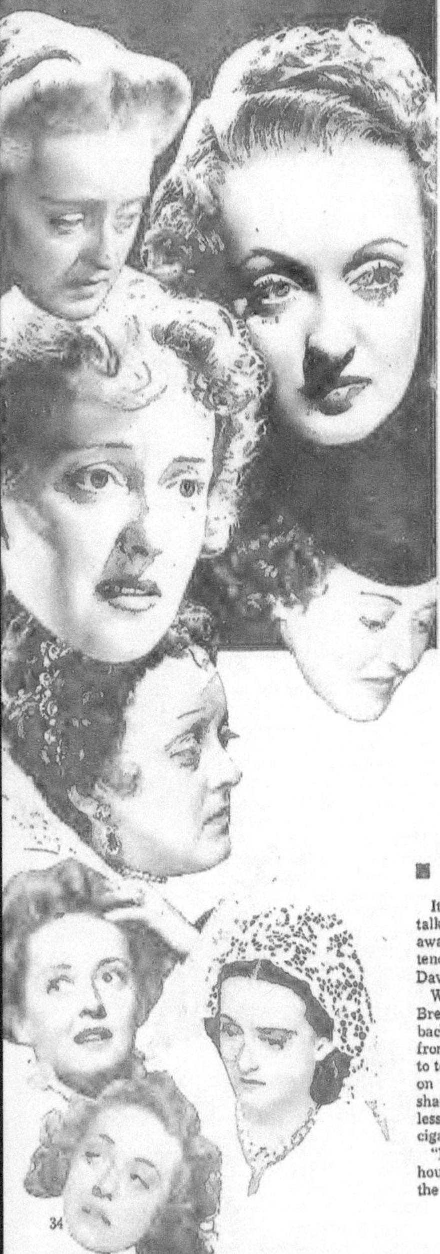

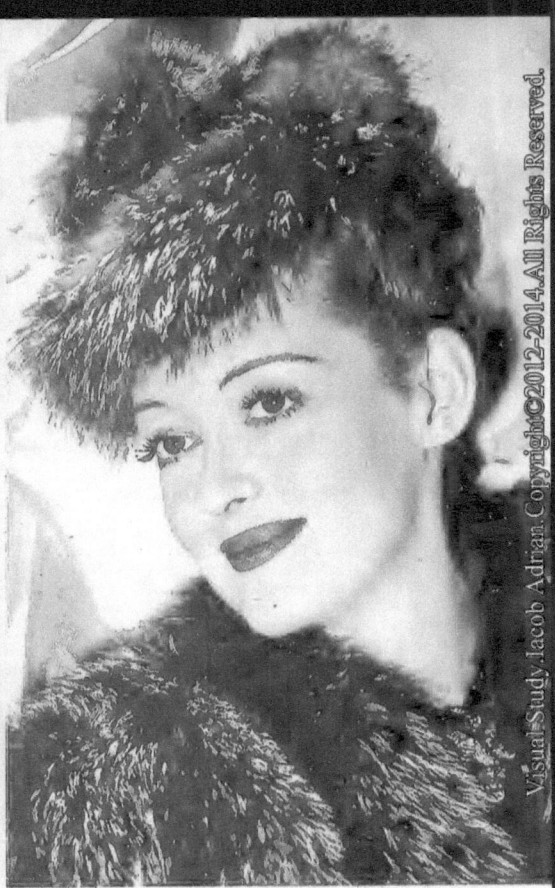

Why Bette Davis fled from Hollywood for a long lazy sojourn in the quiet of New England

By RADIE HARRIS

"You can't count your blessings when you're tired."

It was the First Lady of Hollywood talking—twice honored Academy award winner and, so far leading contender for this year's "Oscar"... Bette Davis to you.

We were sitting in the garden of her Brentwood Heights retreat, now her bachelor quarters since her divorce from "Ham" Nelson. She didn't have to tell me how tired she was. It showed on her pale drawn face—the dark shadows under her eyes—and the restless hands that lit cigarette after cigarette.

"How can I appreciate this lovely house?" Her eyes gazed vacantly at the azaleas in full bloom, the pansy beds that lined the terraced walk leading to the emerald pool. "While I worked on *Elizabeth and Essex*, I was too tired to even come home at night. I lived in my studio dressing room. How can I enjoy my work any more, when it's become just that—work?"

I know I should have reacted with sympathy, but I couldn't suppress a smug grin.

"I know exactly what you're thinking," Bette grinned back at me. "You're remembering a similar conversation we had three summers ago. I was in the same state of nervous exhaustion then, after making *Marked Woman, Kid Galahad, That Certain Woman* and *It's Love I'm After*, and I vowed I'd never allow myself to

34

"Rest Cure" For Bette

Bette Davis — Talent Scout

get into such a condition again."

"I hate to rub it in, but your exact words, if I remember correctly, were, 'No work of any kind—whether it is at the Warner Studios in Burbank—or a factory in Allentown, is worth risking your health for—it's an empty glory being the richest actress in the grave!' "

Bette blew a smoke ring in my direction. "Remind me never to tell you anything I ever want you to forget! Seriously though, I deserve to have you rub it in, because I'm just as stupid as a child who plays with fire once and gets burned, and then does it all over again. I knew I was completely done in, after making *Jezebel, The Sisters, Dark Victory, Juarez* and *The Old Maid* in rapid succession, with no breathing space in between. And yet, I took on *The Private Lives of Elizabeth and Essex.*"

"Why?"

"Because I just can't resist a good part. So what happened? I burst several blood vessels in the process of trying to pitch my voice several tones lower, to affect the robust woman that 'Lizzie' was. And I lost pounds, buried under the weight of the costumes and heavy jewelry."

"What you need is an orgy of rest and relaxation—as far away from Hollywood as you can get," was my parting thrust as I left her in the fading sunlight.

The curtain will now be lowered four times, to denote the lapse of a month. Like a lap-dissolve in a movie, the scene fades into a small New England cottage in Dennis on Cape Cod, Massachusetts. In the driveway is parked a station wagon with a California license. Someone emerges from the doorway and climbs into the driver's seat. She is wearing shorts, sandals. Her yellow hair is flying. Her smile is vivid, care-free. Her blue eyes are as clear as nearby Lake Scargo, and her whole body radiates healthy vitality. I stare incredulously.

"Pardon me, are you *really* Bette Davis?" a timid young thing with an autograph book in her hand asks my unspoken thought. Bette signs obligingly, and then turns to me with a gleeful chuckle.

"You see, I took your advice and got as far away from Hollywood as I could. And what did I find? New faces like Glenda Farrell, Sally Eilers, Doug Montgomery and Don Terry, all straight from Hollywood! They're playing here at the Cape Playhouse in summer stock. Hop in and I'll drive you over to the theatre."

It was less than a five minute ride, but within that short space of time Bette's conversation was like a non-stop exclamation point.

". . . And I put my station wagon on the *Chief* . . . and Peggy Ogden met me at Cornwall. We started acting at Dennis together . . . and Raymond Moore, he gave me my first job here—offered me his guest house . . . and I've always wanted to come back . . . and I haven't read a Hollywood column . . . and I've never

mander of an Irish regiment which kept getting shunted all over the globe. You know how the sun never sets on the British possessions.

He spent his youth tagging along with his father and the Irish regiment, settled down long enough to enroll at flossy Wellington College, then to Sandhurst Military Academy where his best chum was a hell-raiser named, David Niven.

After Sandhurst he tried the military life, found it dull, "chucked it," and went into the trades which he found even more dull. He took off for South Africa where he became a rancher. He was one helluva flop as a rancher.

This was the last straw. So he quit business altogether. As it happened, a sizable sum had been left him by his father. He promptly set out on a life of lazy leisure. Someone told him that California was nifty for all-year-round polo playing, so he hurried right over. That was in 1934.

He had a bang-up time in California— polo, horseback riding and the like. After six months of the leisurely life he went back to England. The first day back in London he ran into Director Edmund Goulding who told him he ought to be in Hollywood making pictures.

"But I've just come from Hollywood," Sutton explained.

"But you must return," Goulding exclaimed.

He returned when he got around to it, was offered a test for a lead in *Only Yesterday,* met a beautiful lady named Charlotte Meier, a nonprofessional, married her, went off to Mexico and stayed there until his money ran out, and returned to Hollywood.

In time he managed to snag a bit in *Last of the Mohicans,* and a pirouette or two in *Dodsworth.* After that he fooled around in the *Bulldog Drummond* sagas for Paramount until he got bored.

What turned the tide was a morsel he landed in *Robin Hood,* just when he and Susan were thinking about hitch-hiking back to England. All he had to do was to gallop up a hill, deliver a message, dismount with zip, deliver a message and gallop down the hill again.

Seven months later when he called around at Warner's to ask if they could use him for a few days, the casting director looked him in the eye and said:

"Oh, you're the one who gallops so beautifully, aren't you?" Then he handed him the role of the dashing captain of the guard in *Elizabeth and Essex,* Bette Davis playing *Elizabeth.* Not to mention Sutton's benefactress.

As for Susan, she will never forget Bette's good deed if she lives to be twenty. If there is anything Susan likes better than eating, she is keeping it quiet, as a well-bred great Dane would. At this writing it looks as if Susan will never have to worry about involuntary dieting again. Not that Susan can't take it. The point is that dieting takes the sheen out of one's coat. And Susan is a proud one, she is.

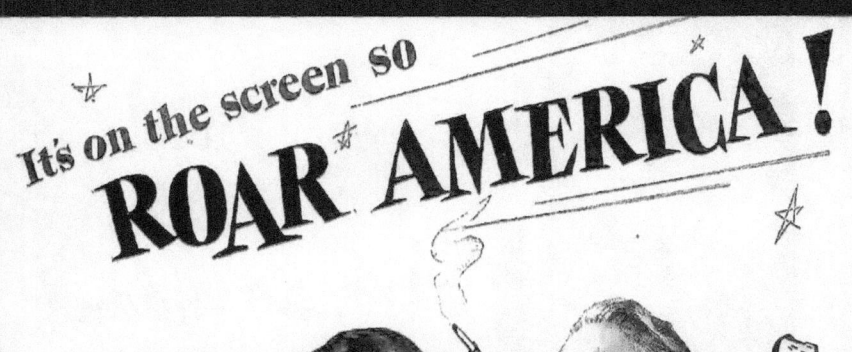

It's on the screen so
ROAR AMERICA!

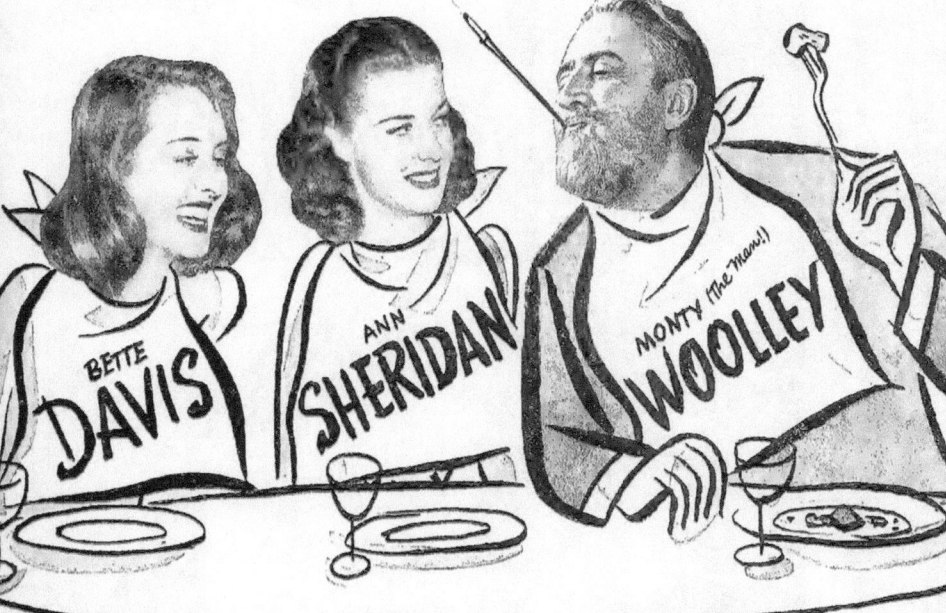

BETTE DAVIS

ANN SHERIDAN

MONTY (the Man!) WOOLLEY

"The Man Who Came to Dinner"

NOTHING COULD BE FUNNIER!

WARNER BROS! NEWEST HIT. With
JIMMY DURANTE • RICHARD TRAVIS
BILLIE BURKE • REGINALD GARDINER
Directed by WILLIAM KEIGHLEY
Screen Play by Julius J. & Philip G. Epstein
From the 2-year-run stage success by
GEO. S. KAUFMAN and MOSS HART
Produced by Sam H. Harris

Your theatre manager will
tell you the opening date..
that's your night to howl!

Bette Davis!

Ann Sheridan!

Monty Woolley!
(He's the man)

Jimmy Durante!

There never was a better reason for "going to the movies" ...'cause there never was a better movie to go to!

The most laughed-at play of our day—with this wonderful Warner Bros. cast *(including the play's celebrated star)* to make it even greater as a picture!

'THE MAN WHO CAME TO DINNER'

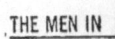

sister against sister!

Love made them hate ⊲—— each other!

THE MEN IN   THEIR LIVES

BETTE SAYS:
"What I want I go after—and I get it!"

OLIVIA SAYS:
"I'm going to be hard—just as hard as she is!"

A sensational novel throbs to life! The cast is one of WARNER BROS' best — the picture is one of Worner Bros.' biggest!

BETTE DAVIS · OLIVIA de HAVILLAND · GEO. BRENT · DENNIS MORGAN

in

"In This Our Life"

with CHARLES COBURN · FRANK CRAVEN · BILLIE BURKE · Directed by John Huston   Screen Play by Howard Koch · Based Upon the Novel by Ellen Glasgow · Music by Max Steiner

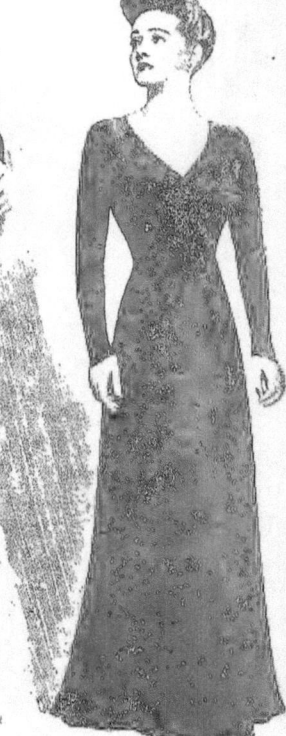

It
happens
in
the best
of
families

But you'd never think it could happen to her!

WARNER BROS.
present their new dramatic triumph
BETTE DAVIS
more exciting, more radiant than ever—with her new co-star
PAUL HENREID
in
Now, Voyager

A story that surpasses
'Stella Dallas', by its
author, Olive Higgins Prouty

A HAL B. WALLIS
PRODUCTION
with
CLAUDE RAINS

GLADYS COOPER · BONITA GRANVILLE · ILKA CHASE · Directed by IRVING RAPPER · Music by Max Steiner · Screen Play by Casey Robinson

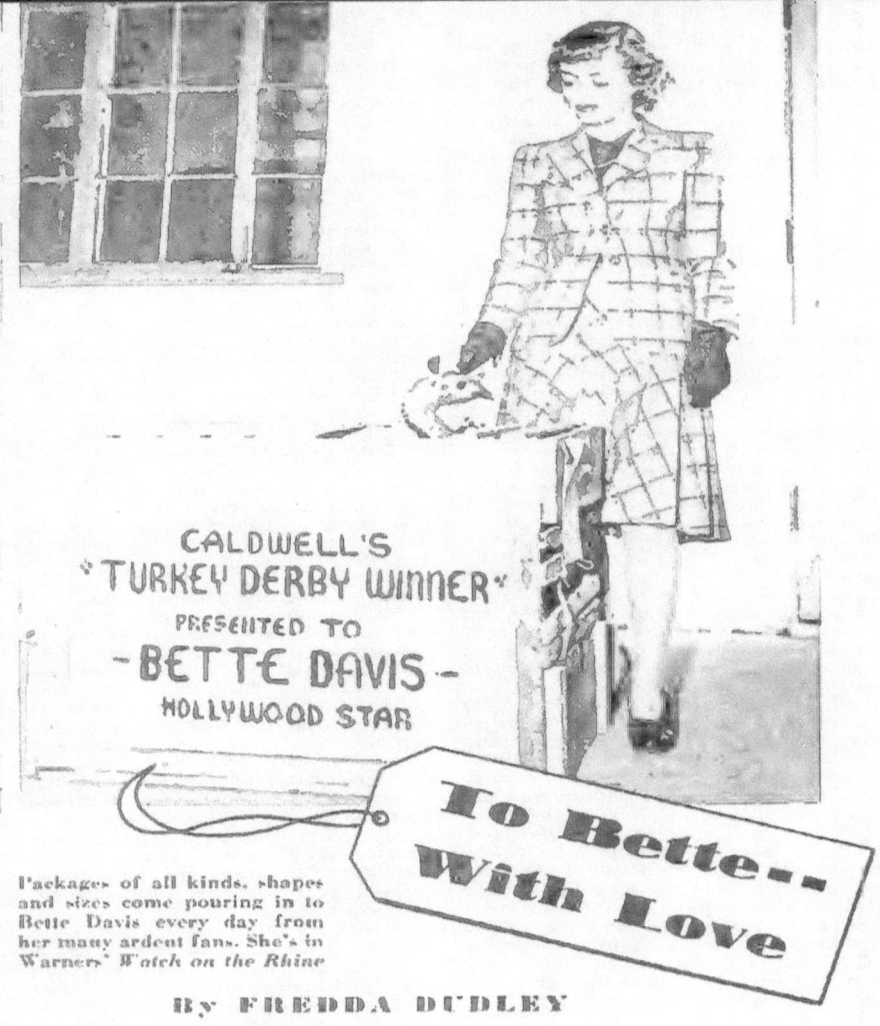

CALDWELL'S
"TURKEY DERBY WINNER"
PRESENTED TO
-BETTE DAVIS-
HOLLYWOOD STAR

To Bette--With Love

Packages of all kinds, shapes and sizes come pouring in to Bette Davis every day from her many ardent fans. She's in Warners' *Watch on the Rhine*

By FREDDA DUDLEY

The square, rather light parcel was delivered to Bette Davis, who forwarded it—with an eyebrow lifted by misgivings—to Bridget Price, her extraordinary secretary.

Mrs. Price tore off the outer wrappings and beheld a sinister black box. In one side there was a small, circular opening, and from this protruded a length of cord, which strongly resembled a fuse despite a card tacked on the top of the box reading, "To Bette With Love."

Mrs. Price shook the package carefully and grew alarmed at the sound. "It's a bomb," she decided in one breath while calling the police in the next. Three good men and true from the Bomb Squad came screeching over to investigate. First they saturated the package with a hose, then one bold fellow gingerly lifted the lid.

No sticks of dynamite. No TNT. Not even a package of firecrackers. In the box was a carved wooden dog with a formidable leash about his neck. Said leash was pulled through the hole in the box. Apparently an ardent fan of Bette's had sculped the dog, then added the tether as a gag, thereby nearly scaring several people completely out of their wits.

This is just a sample of the weird and wonderful collection of gifts that constantly pours into her studio for the popular actress. Several months ago, a man in Montana wrote to say that he had captured a prize mountain lion and that he was shipping it to Hollywood at once, thinking it would make a nice pet—after it had been given a manicure. Bette disagreed, and wired her friend many thanks, with a request to set the animal free . . . or give him to a museum.

At Thanksgiving time last year she was the astonished and delighted recipient of a prize turkey. Not just an ordinary bird, you understand, but a patrician gobbler that had won a derby in his district.

Speaking of animals, a gentleman who crosses dogs and monkeys sent Bette a sample offspring of this fanciful union. When the poor thing arrived it was dead, but Bette took a look at it anyhow to see what the beast looked like. After several solemn moments, Bette sighed, "Sometimes I think Nature is entirely too grand."

Bette's birthday—April 5th—is always the signal for an avalanche of presents. From Mexico she has received beautiful silver bracelets—solid semi-circles with elaborate carving, as well as intertwined silver links. From Italy—posted just before war broke out and considerably delayed in transit—she received a fragile Venetian blown-glass vase. It wasn't broken!

From South America she receives tiny moccasins to be worn as lapel ornaments, beaded miniature chaps, and small vividly dressed dolls. At least once a month she receives small handmade sombreros to be worn on suits. As for America—all over this broad land there are earnest hands crocheting roses, or making golliwogs out of wool, or tinting pictures to be sent to "Miss Bette Davis, Hollywood."

For Christmas last year, the Davis Fan Club sent Bette 3,000 initialed hankies. Some were embroidered with a simple "B" or "D," but occasionally an admirer chose the letter "F" for Farnsworth. Bette spent nearly a week, opening packages in her spare time. She loved them all.

Think not that the fans of Miss Davis stop at handkerchief showers, lapel gadgets, homemade jewelry or carving. Their generosity leaps on to such household items as luncheon sets, hooked rugs, and tufted bedspreads. A year never goes by in which Bette doesn't receive dozens of these items. Too, she receives literally hundreds of letters from the nimble-fingered who have made luncheon sets, hooked rugs and tufted bedspreads, and who would like to sell them to Bette.

Not only does she receive table linen, but things to go on the table as well. She gets pound after pound of fruit cake throughout the year. During the holiday season she could pave her dressing room with pastry. And candy! America is filled with makers of prize divinity, penuche, fudge, and fondant. Even the sugar shortage hasn't daunted many a genius of the copper kettle because sweets still arrive by the pound.

Most impressive gift of candy arrived on the set of *Now, Voyager* from a man who had made an "Oscar" out of chocolate and awarded it to her for her work in *The Little Foxes* which he had just seen.

She receives still another type of gift—one that she regards very highly. Occasionally someone, usually an older woman, has no one to whom to bequeath a particular treasure. There was, for instance, the case of the Maine dowager who wrote in a fine Spencerian hand, "My dear Miss Davis: As I am eighty-eight years of age, I know I have not many years more to spend in this world. I have disposed of all my possessions with the exception of the enclosed naval buttons, cuff links, and dress-uniform belt. They belonged to my grandson—a fine boy who gave his life for his country. You were always his favorite actress, so I want you to have these priceless keepsakes."

Bette has the insignia tucked away with other treasured mementos of her career.

Less tear-inspiring was another bequest she received some time ago. She was notified by Railway Express that an item of furniture consigned to her was waiting at the Los Angeles freight depot. Thoroughly mystified, Bette insisted that she had ordered no furniture. "I think you have the wrong Bette Davis," she hazarded.

"Don't think so," said the agent. " 'Miss Bette Davis, Warner Brothers Studio, Hollywood,' the tag says. Must be you."

Bette inveigled two of the boys from the transportation department to drive down and have a look-see. Convinced, they brought the gift out to the studio. It was an old-fashioned, hand-carved, three-sectional solid oak bookcase. Small busts of Shakespeare decorated each terminal post of the massive affair, and the doors were important with plate glass.

A few days later Bette received a letter of explanation from an elderly Massachusetts fan. Seems Old Ironsides had been in the donor's family for generations, but the blood line was dying with this particular little old lady . . . so she had decided to send the heirloom to Bette.

Bette, a little staggered—but grateful—had it shipped to her New England farm.

Big gifts, little gifts. Funny, serious, heartrending, useless, valuable—all sizes, kinds and conditions of presents keep pouring in, so Bette has a message for her fans everywhere:

"I wish I could thank every one of you personally for the lovely things you have sent me. I'm so grateful for your generosity and thoughtfulness. To be honest, I like to receive tokens of esteem as well as anyone on earth. But to all my kind friends who may want to send me some remembrance in the future, I would like to say this: Nothing will make me happier than for you to use any small sum you may plan to spend on a present for me toward buying War Bonds and Stamps. In that way, we will both be contributing some small part to our nation's war effort, and to preserving the way of life that means so much to us all. Will you do this for me?"

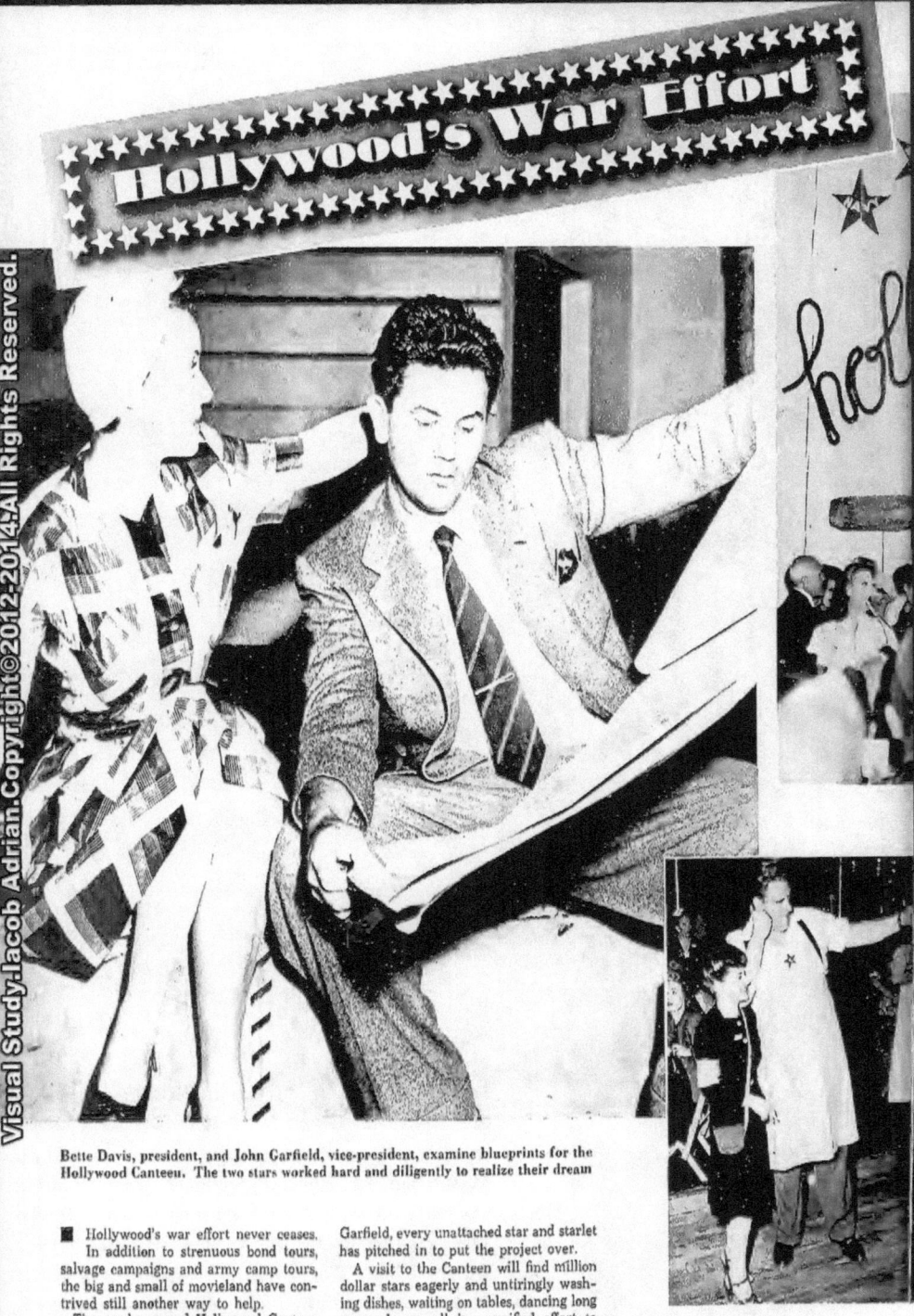

Hollywood's War Effort

Bette Davis, president, and John Garfield, vice-president, examine blueprints for the Hollywood Canteen. The two stars worked hard and diligently to realize their dream

■ Hollywood's war effort never ceases.

In addition to strenuous bond tours, salvage campaigns and army camp tours, the big and small of movieland have contrived still another way to help.

The newly opened Hollywood Canteen is being operated as a recreation center for U. S. servicemen.

Together with Bette Davis and John Garfield, every unattached star and starlet has pitched in to put the project over.

A visit to the Canteen will find million dollar stars eagerly and untiringly washing dishes, waiting on tables, dancing long weary hours—all in a unified effort to make America's fighting men feel at home.

It is justifiably Hollywood's pride and joy. ■

Mammoth-sized Laird Cregar and a petite hostess relax a moment before the crowd arrives

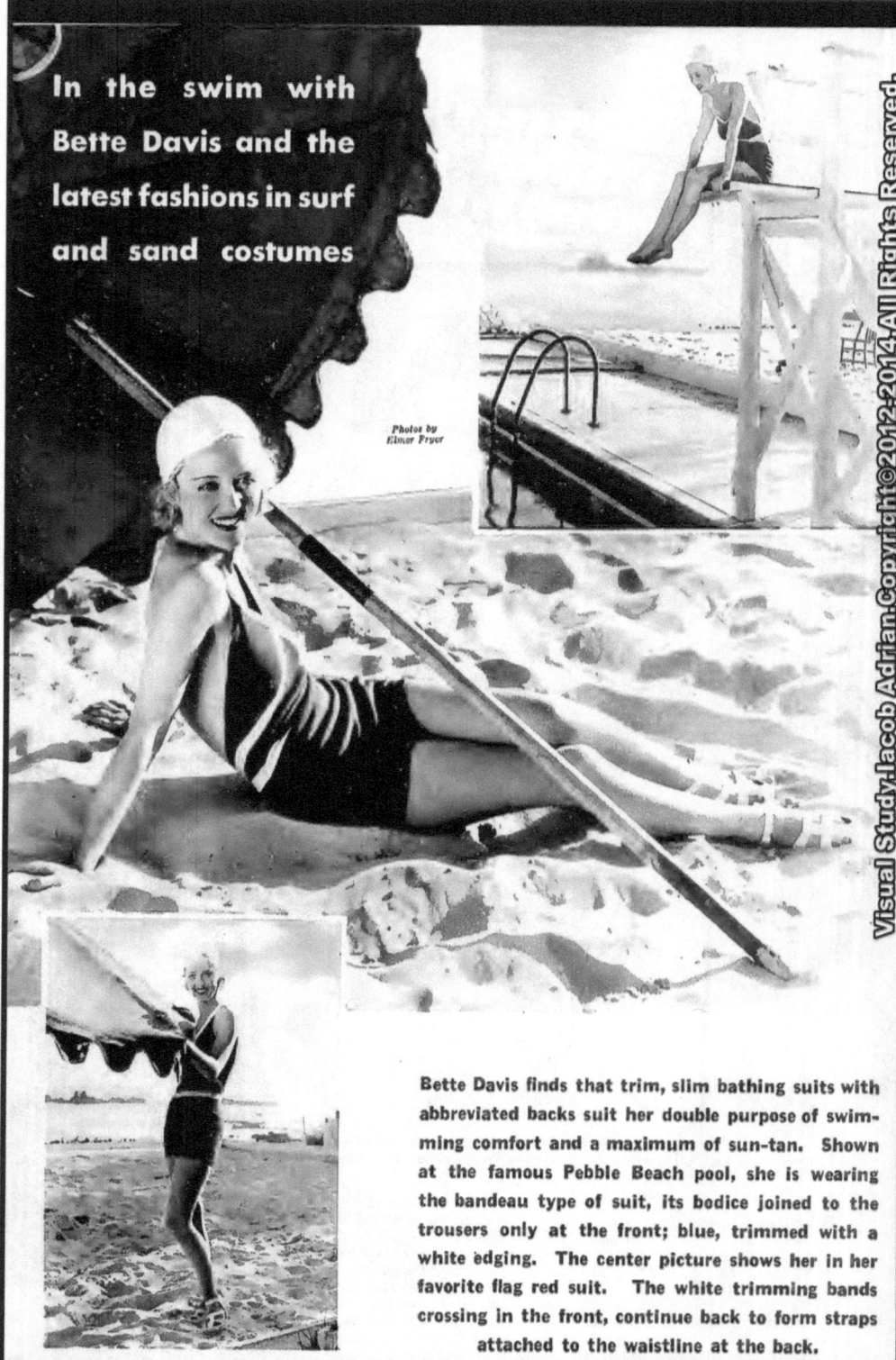

In the swim with Bette Davis and the latest fashions in surf and sand costumes

Photos by Elmer Fryer

Bette Davis finds that trim, slim bathing suits with abbreviated backs suit her double purpose of swimming comfort and a maximum of sun-tan. Shown at the famous Pebble Beach pool, she is wearing the bandeau type of suit, its bodice joined to the trousers only at the front; blue, trimmed with a white edging. The center picture shows her in her favorite flag red suit. The white trimming bands crossing in the front, continue back to form straps attached to the waistline at the back.

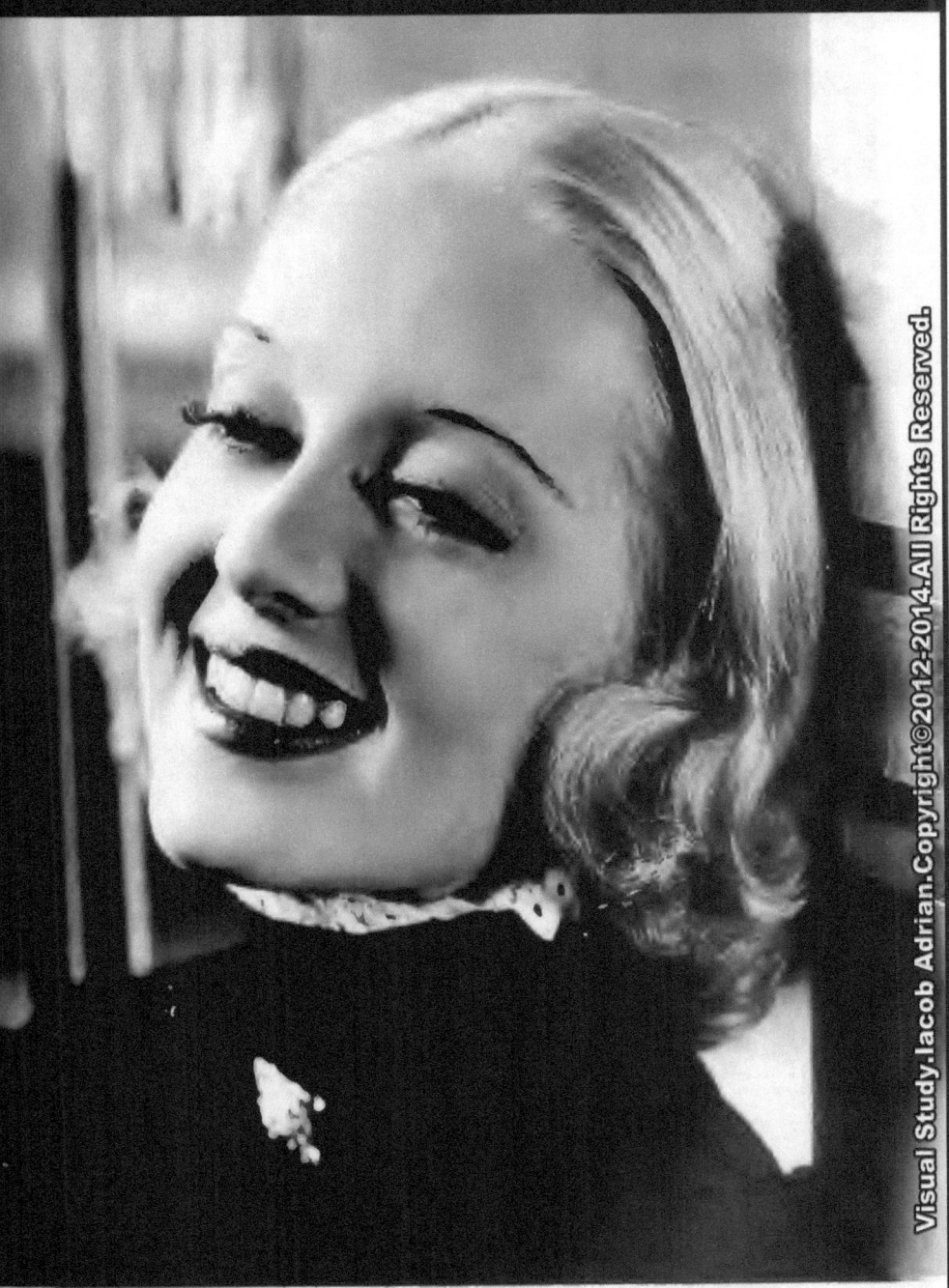

Bert Longworth

BETTE DAVIS—Forgot early desire to be a nurse in high school eagerness for stage career. Studied with John Murray Anderson. Given initial opportunity in George Cukor's stock company. Then to Broadway. Made good in several plays. Hollywood beckoned, and a Universal contract. No luck—option dropped. Bette changed her disposition; turned snappy instead of sweet. A Warner contract and flicker fame! Married to Harmon O. Nelson.

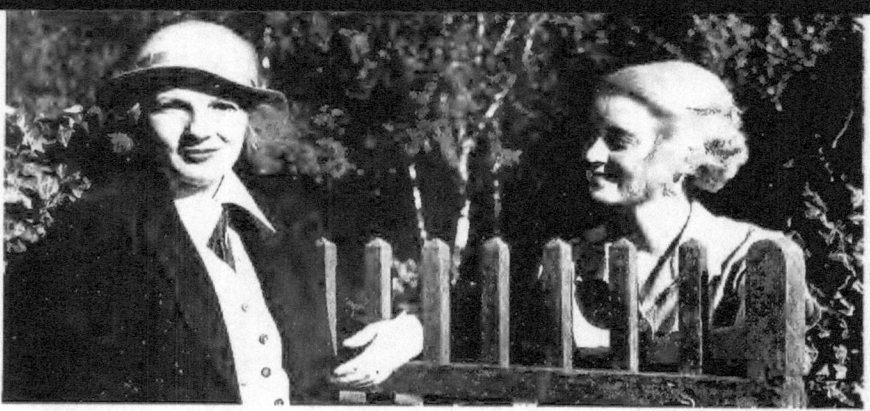

Chatting over the back fence—Bette and Martha Ford. Martha knows about actors; she married one.

BETTE DAVIS
from
New England

Some say she is willful. Bette thinks she's spoiled; but she is courageously determined to Martha Ford, her old friend and neighbor

BETTE DAVIS has become, virtually overnight, a young lady of some importance. But she's still the same Bette Davis who went early to bed, the night before the now momentous opening of "Of Human Bondage."

And twenty years from now, a little older, a bit less youthfully blonde, but every bit as dynamic, she'll still be Bette Davis. You can change the course of a mountain spring but you can't change the purity of the water. She may have learned to express her opinions a shade more fearlessly in the years between the time she began to develop herself as a person and now, but you can be perfectly certain that those opinions, though dormant, have always been basically the same. Bette's a New Englander. You can dress a New Englander up like the Lilies of the Field, but he remains at bottom a slightly hide-bound, principled, courageous, ambitious, God-fearing, worldly-wise but straight-marching conservative.

Bette and I have known each other a good many years, as friendships go, but, in all that time, I've never known her to be in any way other than herself. I'll admit, and Bette will admit, that she has developed a more "glammy" exterior, but her ideas and ideals—ah, shades of Ruthie, the grandest of all mothers—are today as they were yesterday and as they will be tomorrow.

She has all the determination and "drive," of the creatures on earth, in the sea, in heaven and under the earth. She's stubborn as a mule and sweet as the early dew. You can lead her, with reason and understanding, into any "dark forest"—but try to drive her, even into "Primrose Paths"! There are those who say she's willful—I say she's

Wide World Photos

courageously determined—she says she's spoiled. The result is a young woman of glorious singleness of purpose. Fight she will and weep she can, but turn back, never!

Belying the far-famed New England conscience and fear of witchcraft in all its forms, Betty adores things wild and woolly. A howling wind, a darkened room and Edgar Allen Poe, read under difficulty in the semi-darkness, are her meat. Oh, the fun we've had with spirit writings from "Planchette"! We don't really believe, down in our hearts, but for days, we look fearfully behind us at the sound of Little Footsteps—and the sudden banging of a door has been

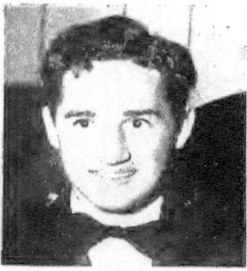

Bette's husband, Harmon (Ham) O. Nelson, the toy band and the elephants which glowed at night and made him think he had D. T.'s.

known to throw us into delicious hysteria. Even smart girls, like us'ns, like to be "spooked" every now and then. I'll never forget the night—but that's beside the point. Sufficient it is to say that our Bette put her conscience in cold-storage and let the "other world" have its way with us!

She has lived in two of Charlie Farrell's houses. What's good enough for one New Englander is good enough for another, Boston or Cape Cod notwithstanding. Both houses are as distinctly Bette as they are Charlie—passively English, beautifully complete, with touches of a forgivable "capitalism" here and there in the form of deep, deep rugs and very old "objets d'art."

But Bette sleeps in Ham's pajamas, in her taffeta and lace bed, and Ham's pajamas are only just pajamas. They're a size and again too large for Bette and it leaves poor Ham a little short at the end of the week. But those two sublime idiots adore each other. If ever I've seen a really fifty-fifty marriage, theirs is *it*. Ham won't and doesn't have to live on Bette's money and Bette won't and doesn't have to live on Ham's. The answer to the equation being a pooling of interests that has Solomon beat all hollow. They make each other sentimental but crazy little presents.

Ham's a musician, and the other day Bette bought four little men with musical instruments made of wood, for Ham's own private orchestra. But she also bought two tiny elephants filled with phosphorus, that gleamed wickedly in the night. She decided that the pink elephants would make a better show as a surprise on Ham's night-table, so she switched them. Suddenly, in the middle

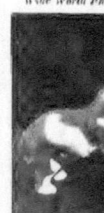

Bette Davis from New England

of the night, there they were,—the pink and luminous elephants. And though he knew there wasn't any reason to be seeing them—there they were. He decided to ignore them. They simply *couldn't* exist. And in ignoring them, he spoiled a great joke. Next morning, he sauntered up to Bette and said, "Listen, Davis, wait till I've earned the nocturnal D. T.'s" . . . and Bette, properly crushed but still inventive, pulled out the little orchestra.

Bette and Ham share those domestic kicks under the table that are a true barometer of a companionable and intimate coupling of thoughts. They scold and laugh and weep together . . . if they feel so inclined, and Ham and Bette are like,—well, like ham and eggs,—they somehow just seem to "fit in" together. A lifted eye-brow tells an untold tale—a wide grin holds a joke unshared with any living creature, a sudden cough means, in their secret parlance, "thumbs down." Ham's name is really Nelson and Nelson was, so history has it, the one-armed hero of Trafalgar. Our Nelson may have both his arms, but he is, none the less, the Iron Man of his household. When he says "yes," it's yes. When he says "No,"—well, that often depends on Bette!

Bette is the world's most devoted big sister. Her truly beautiful young sister, Bobbe, has been seriously ill for the past year and Bette has cared for her most tenderly. Bobbe, better now, bless her independent heart, in an attempt to "make up" to Bette for all she's done, has sent her several interesting maps of Hollywood and its environs, sewed in colored threads on a sail-cloth background. She has started a veritable fad in this old town. If Bobbe cared to, she could make a pleasant living with her maps. They'll be worth a lot some day,—more, I think, than the samplers our grandmothers used to make as girls, because they are so infinitely more amusing. Bobbie, in her own way, is as talented as Bette. A little less sure of herself from a commercial standpoint, but I still feel that she'll accomplish a great deal one of these days. And, as for Ruthie—mother of all swell mothers—she'll doubtless have the job of seeing both of her girls riding the crest of the wave, because she has "builded well." Ruthie is a non-possessive mother. As a matter of fact, she doesn't intrude her maternity on her daughters at all. She's far more like a grown sister who cheers the younger ones on to fulfillment, with the dreams of her own aspirations still lingering in her eyes. She's the best friend in the world to have and the most implacable enemy. The whole family, Bette and Ham and Bobbe and Ruthie, seem to have a soldier's agreement to stand shoulder to shoulder, come fire, flood or famine!

Bette is no angel of heavenly disposition. She has a flaring temper and often quick petulance that blossoms, nine times out of ten, into those famous roars of laughter that are noisy enough to wake the dead. She can't manage to stay mad a moment, once you've been able to conjure up those shouts of whole-souled laughter. She's no lady of exotic subtleties, she's herself—laugh and all. She fights anyone's and everyone's battles. She gets sputteringly indignant at injustice and will take on an army in hand-to-hand combat.

Bette has a good deal of vision and courage. She can stand afar off and take stock of herself and when she thinks she needs a good "redding up" Bette can get to work on Bette as though she were someone else entirely. She plans the changes she has made in herself, entirely without suggestions from anyone, but she refuses to experiment. She's sure of the effect she wants to achieve before she starts. But, and this is a most important but, she's never satisfied with her work. She feels if she had *Mildred*, the little cockney waitress in "Bondage," to do over again, there are a hundred and one improvements she could make in her characterization. She thinks she did as well as she could have at the time, but knows that now she could do a better job. That's why Bette will continue to grow artistically—she's eager to learn, willing to work, and never, never satisfied.

She is often, and easily, misquoted, because she thinks so rapidly that, by the time you've caught up with her, your mental notes are sadly garbled. She is so out-and-out frank that she often gives people the wrong impression. Only her friends are capable of judging her. They alone can know and appreciate Bette.

One of the first parts Bette ever played was with my husband, Wallace Ford, in a special engagement of "Broadway," in Rochester, N. Y. As I recall, she hopped into the part of Pearl when the tempestuous lass then playing it suffered a semi-sprained ankle just before the second-act curtain. Bette the Brave, the light of battles shining in her eyes, did as neat a show-saving job as I ever hope to see. She played it so well that when the pseudo-sprained ankle miraculously healed after the matinee, Bette stayed on in the part. Before this Bette trained as a classical dancer, no less! From then on, she left terpsichore to struggle on without her, and turned to the sister art.

B ETTE reads all her own fan-mail and answers the greater part of it herself. It's a goodly task, I might add, because I've helped her with it. She saves and re-reads letters of honest and constructive criticism. She's artistically ambitious to a startling degree. If ever a girl loved and respected her work, that girl is Bette Davis. That's the reason for her occasional tiffs with her studio. She feels that once she'd made a definite step ahead, she should be permitted to retain the ground she's won, and not be forced to slide back into stereotyped roles. She's not afraid of hard work, but she is afraid of bad parts.

To change the subject abruptly, Bette and I waited on table at the Assistance League two weeks ago. When you wait on table at the League, you're a Junior Leaguer, a sub-deb or a Somewhat Important Person. We waited on table—I, being none of the above—I'm used to it. But Bette to all intents and purposes a veritable beginner was fully expected to cave in under the strain. But she took to it like the proverbial duck to water. Everyone waited on, and in, the side-lines did a thorough-going gasping job, but Bette didn't let them flounder in admiration long. "For one solid mortal year," she stated flatly, "I waited table to earn my way through school, and I was a he—ck of a good waitress. I ought to be good. . . !"

And there is Bette Davis . . . my friend and your particular joy in life . . . and the best and smartest blonde in all the world, synthetic or otherwise!

You loved her in "MADAME X"..."SARAH & SON"..."TOMORROW and TOMORROW"

Now see her in ALL her glory...

Miss
Ruth
Chatterton

HER LOVELINESS ENHANCED...
HER MAGIC MULTIPLIED...IN
HER first FIRST NATIONAL PICTURE

The RICH
ARE ALWAYS WITH US

The ultra smart set in the mad scramble for
thrills!...A sumptuous portrayal of sensuous
society in the perfumed fragrance of Park
Avenue and Paris boudoirs...Witty—naughty
—gay!...A spectacular story of how the ritzy
half lives — and loves — and lies...Com-
ing soon to leading theatres everywhere.

COULD THEY CHEAT
THE MARRIAGE GAME?

with BETTE DAVIS
GEORGE BRENT   JOHN MILJAN
Direction by
ALFRED E. GREEN

another FIRST NATIONAL *Hit!*

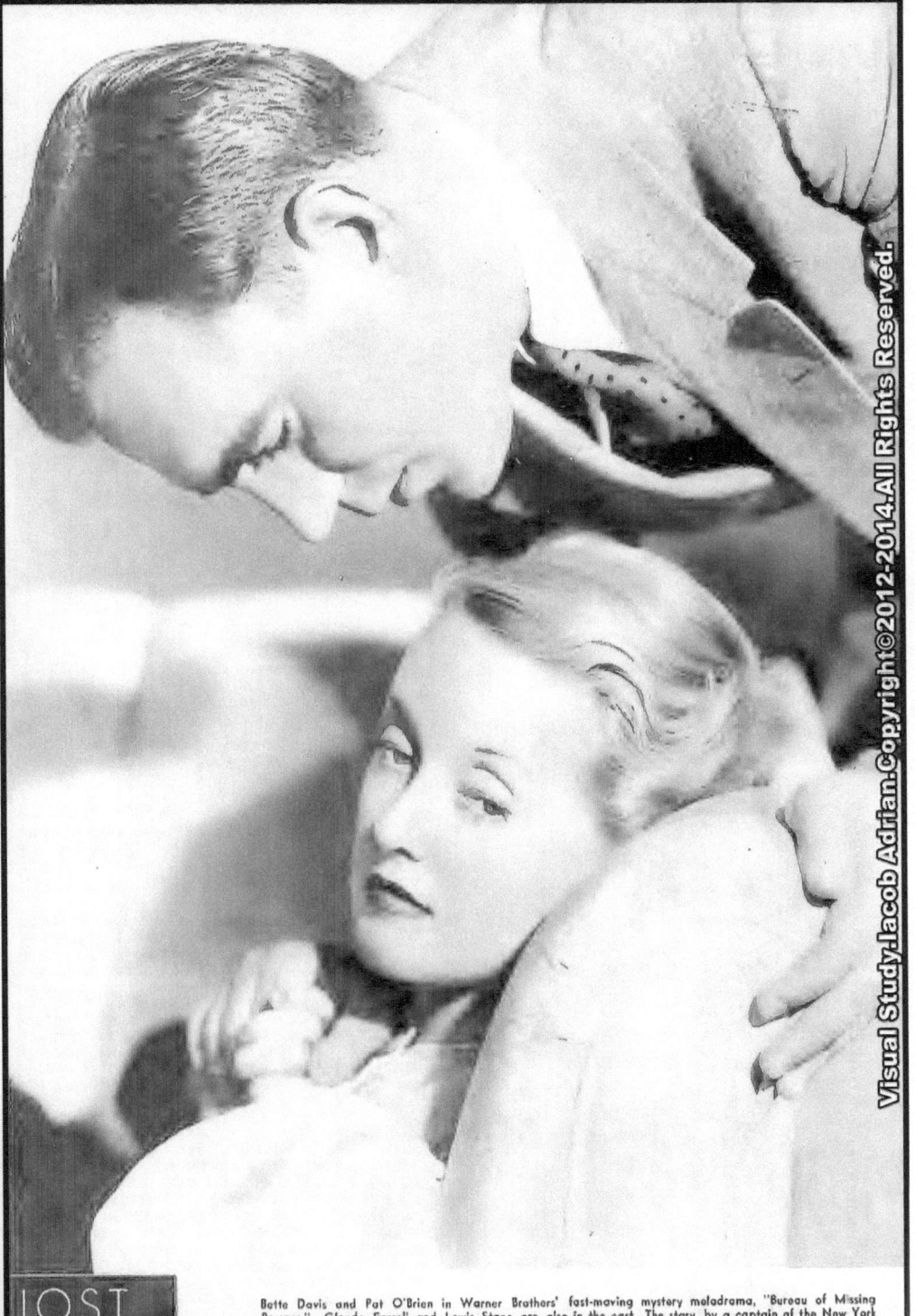

LOST

Bette Davis and Pat O'Brien in Warner Brothers' fast-moving mystery melodrama, "Bureau of Missing Persons." Glenda Farrell and Lewis Stone are also in the cast. The story, by a captain of the New York police, tells of the search for the thousands of persons who drop into oblivion each year.

NEW LIPS
IN HOLLYWOOD

Girls like Bette Davis adopt a more convincing use of lip make-up

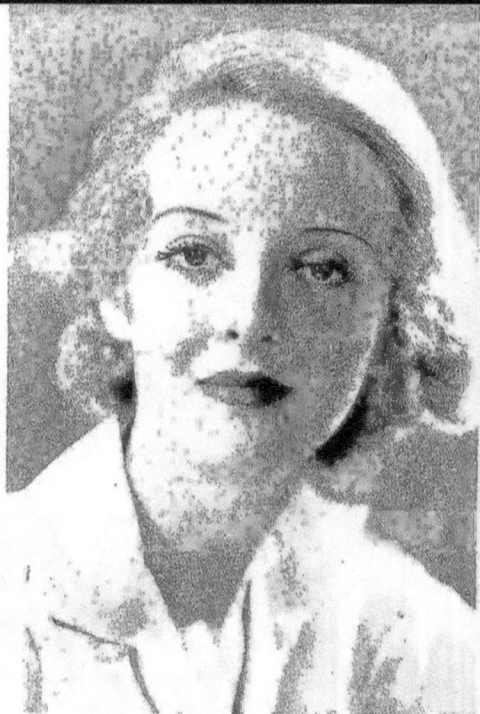

Personality portrait by Elmer Fryer

So you have heard they aren't using much lipstick in Hollywood. We have too, but it is not precisely true, because girls who set the styles in motion pictures are making as liberal use as ever of lipstick, rouge and other cosmetics designed to improve the lips. But they are using it more adroitly. They realize that off the screen it should be applied so as to bring out the natural contours of the lips instead of serving as a glaring red mask over the mouth, and when making up for the screen the wide exaggerated lipstick is used only when that type of make-up suits the character portrayed. Bette Davis provides a good example of this newer use of lip cosmetics. Off screen, she uses the lighter make-up that reveals the elusive charm of her own lovely lips. In her recent depiction of Mildred in Warner Brothers' "Of Human Bondage" she appears with the exaggerated lip make-up that fits the character of Mildred.

You know how it was a few years ago—off the stage as well as on. Whatever prejudices there were against the use of this form of cosmetic had disappeared, so we used it with the lavish hand of a child dipping into the new box of water-

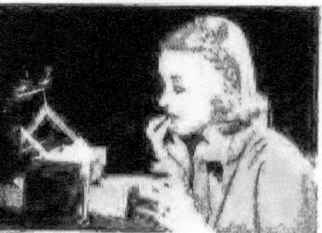

● Bette Davis of Warner Brothers and First National with lighter make-up.

● She takes time between shots to beautify her lips.

colors. Red lips were the fashion. They made us look strong and brave and we thought they made us look young and beautiful. Screen stars followed, or led the fashion. We got used to it, just as we get used to any other fashion—knee-length skirts or green enameled fingernails.

One or two of the stars went in so heavily for this exaggerated effect that in some cases, now that the reaction has set in in favor of more subtly made-up lips, orders have been issued from studio headquarters to destroy the old photographs showing the thick over-made-up lips with the hope that the dear Public will forget. Sure enough they are gone—but not forgotten, and the remembrance of them contrasted with the present subtler use of lip cosmetics will help us not to repeat the mistake.

But don't let the edict for more delicately colored lips lead to negligence. In our own opinion lip make-up, even when it is over-done, is one of the most valuable of all cosmetics uses. The immediate purpose of it all is naturally to improve the shape and color of the lips, but aside from that the regular use of good lipstick keeps the lips soft and smooth, preventing chapped, rough lips that were one of the usual cold weather beauty problems of girls in the pre-lipstick era.

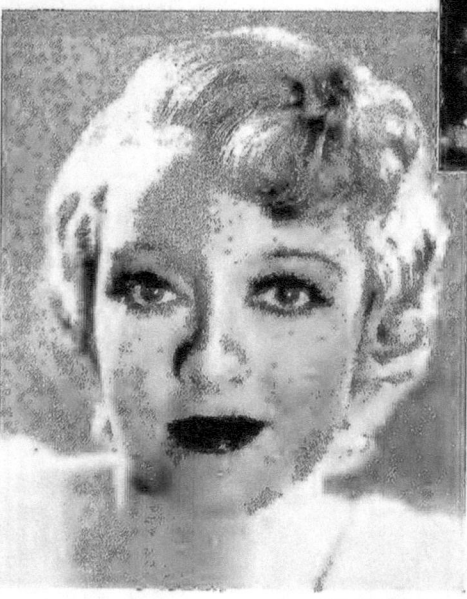

Photo by Bret Longworth

● A one-sided bang and a wide coating of heavy lip make-up give an entirely different expression to Bette Davis's lovely face.

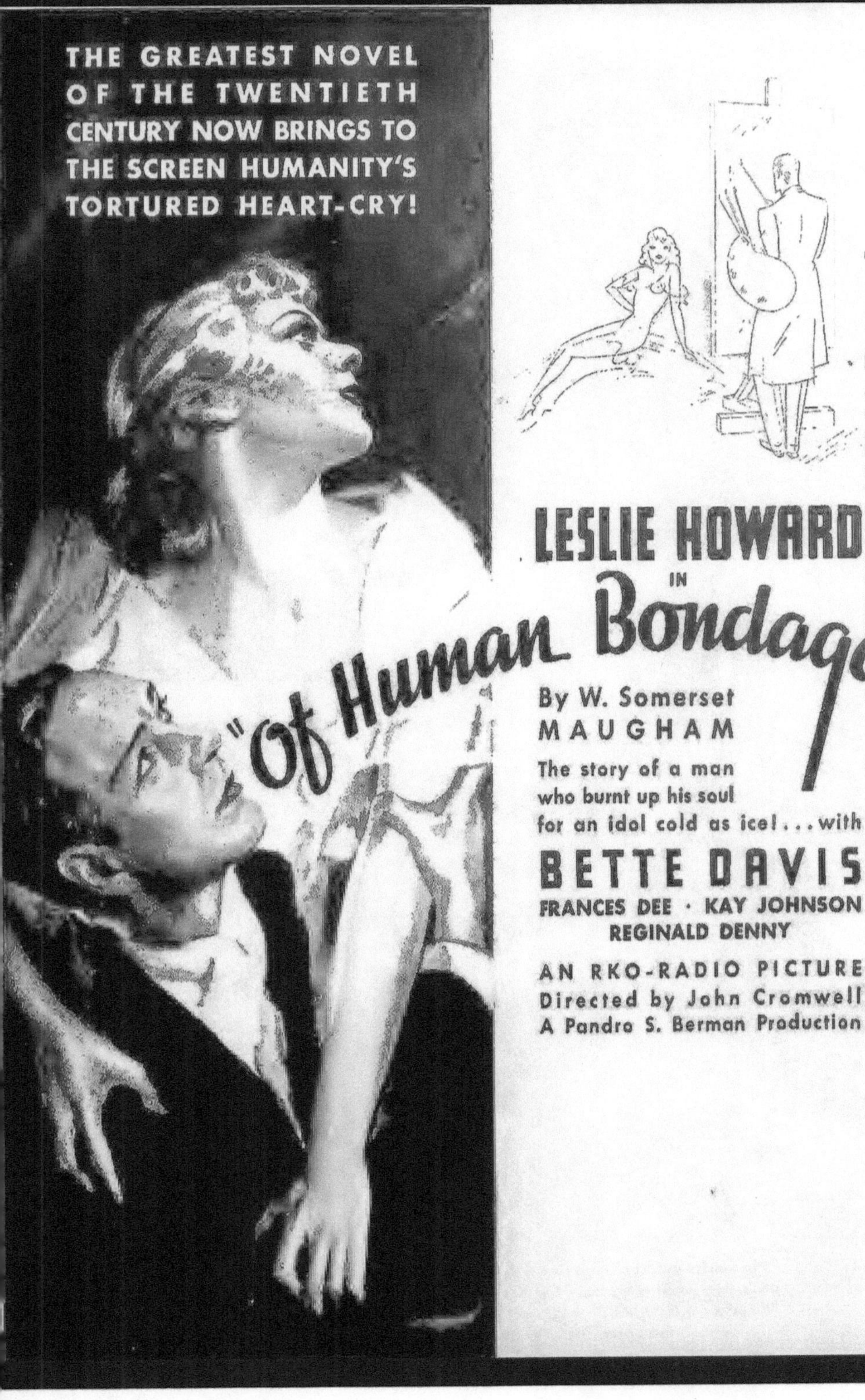

THE GREATEST NOVEL
OF THE TWENTIETH
CENTURY NOW BRINGS TO
THE SCREEN HUMANITY'S
TORTURED HEART-CRY!

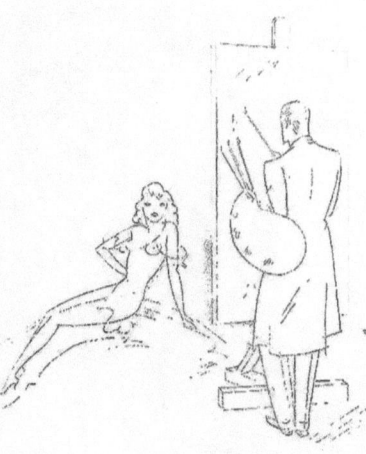

LESLIE HOWARD
IN
"Of Human Bondage"

By W. Somerset
MAUGHAM
The story of a man
who burnt up his soul
for an idol cold as ice!...with

BETTE DAVIS
FRANCES DEE · KAY JOHNSON
REGINALD DENNY

AN RKO-RADIO PICTURE
Directed by John Cromwell
A Pandro S. Berman Production

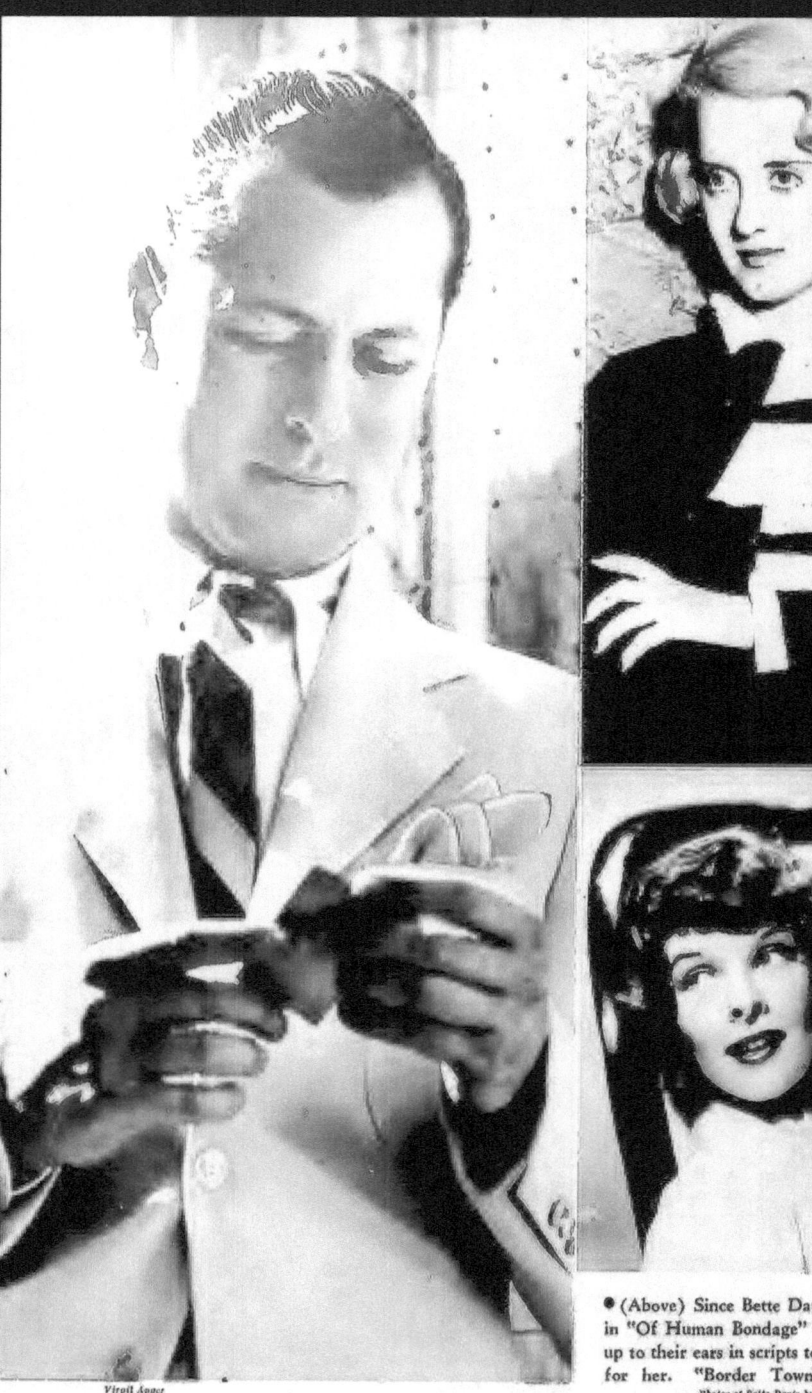

Photo by Ernest A. Bachrach

● (Above) Since Bette Davis made such a hit in "Of Human Bondage" Warners have been up to their ears in scripts to find a suitable one for her. "Border Town" was the choice.

Photos of Bette Davis by Elmer Fryer

● (Below) Katharine Hepburn seems all agog about something. She's probably thrilled about playing "Babbie," the Gypsy girl, in Barrie's well-beloved play, "The Little Minister."

Virgil Apger

● No wonder Robert Montgomery is a good actor! They don't seem to write scenarios fast enough for him. In "Forsaking All Others," you'll see him teamed once more with Joan Crawford.

Bibliographic sources :

Hollywood (1934-1943)
Publisher: Hollywood Magazine, inc. ; Fawcett Publications, inc.

The New Movie Magazine 1930 - 1935
Publisher: Tower Magazines, inc.

This documentary study use,
combined in various proportions,
elements from the following categories,
forms and subsets :
- fair use
- documentary
- documentary photography
- feature
- journalism
- arts journalism
- visual journalism
- photojournalism
- celebrity photography
in order to :
- employ material as the object of cultural critique ,
- quote to illustrate an argument or point ,
- use material in historical sequence,
providing independent opinion,
using photos, press articles, advertisements,
opinions of fans etc. ...